MISRULE

Politicians tend to be like starlings going from one perch to another. Time moves on. The *dramatis personae* of public life change. Some die. Others go to the House of Lords. Others to the obscurity of private life. Those who remain in public life change jobs. Accountability for yesterday's actions is difficult to pinpoint. That's why ministers get away with so much. But one minister has not been subject to retirement or musical chairs. She is the Prime Minister. And there is one aspect of the events described in this book which should not be history. That is truthfulness or non-truthfulness to the House of Commons. Those who practise deceit on the House of Commons, and when that seems to fail, go further and brazenly lie their way out of trouble (as Mrs Thatcher lied in the Westland affair), are not worthy to hold great offices of State, let alone lead this country.

About the Author

Tam Dalyell was once suspended from the House for unparliamentary behaviour when he referred to the Prime Minister as 'a bounder, a liar, a deceiver, a cheat and a crook'. He has been a Member of Parliament for twenty-six years and a member of the Public Accounts Committee from 1962–66. Between 1966–70 he was PPS to the late Dick Crossman and Member of the European Parliament from 1976–79. He was the Labour Party spokesman on science until Michael Foot sacked him during the Falklands conflict for his opposition to the conduct of the war. He has been a weekly columnist for the *New Scientist* for twenty years and was the first Scot ever to be elected by the Constituency Labour Parties to the National Executive Committee of the Labour Party.

Misrule

How Mrs Thatcher has misled Parliament from the Sinking of the Belgrano to the Wright Affair

---

Tam Dalyell, MP

NEW ENGLISH LIBRARY
Hodder and Stoughton

Copyright © 1987 by Tam Dalyell

First published in Great Britain in 1987 by Hamish Hamilton Limited

New English Library Paperback edition 1988

British Library C.I.P.

Dalyell, Tam
   Misrule: how Mrs Thatcher has misled Parliament from the sinking of the Belgrano to the Wright affair.
   1. Great Britain – Politics and government – 1979–
   I. Title
   320.941   JN231

   ISBN 0-450-42488-X

Printed and bound in Great Britain for Hodder and Stoughton Paperbacks, a division of Hodder and Stoughton Limited, Mill Road, Dunton Green, Sevenoaks, Kent (Editorial Office: 47 Bedford Square, London WC1B 3DP) by Richard Clay Limited, Bungay, Suffolk. Photoset by Rowland Phototypesetting Limited, Bury St Edmunds, Suffolk.

Contents

Dedication

Misrule is dedicated to all the Constituency Labour Parties who have invited me to speak at public meetings – some 260 of them – over a period when a lot of other people, some of whom should have known better, dismissed my charges against Mrs Thatcher as 'over the top'. They are:

Aldershot, Aldridge Brownhills, Alyn and Deeside, Argyll and Bute, Arundel, Ashford, Ashton-under-Lyne, Ayr, Banff and Buchan, Barnsley, Barrow-in-Furness, Basingstoke, Bath, Battersea, Beaconsfield, Bedfordshire Mid, Berkshire East, Bexleyheath, Birkenhead, Birmingham City Parties, Blaby, Bootle, Bradford City Party, Brent South, Brentwood and Ongar, Brigg and Cleethorpes, Brighton Kemptown, Bristol East, Bristol West, Broxbourne, Buckingham, Burton, Bury North, Bury St Edmunds, Caithness and Sutherland, Calder Valley, Cambridge, Cambridgeshire South East, Canterbury, Cardiff South and Penarth, Carlisle, Carmarthen, Chelmsford, Chelsea, Chesham and Amersham, Chester, Chesterfield, Chorley, Christchurch, Cirencester and Tewkesbury, City of London and Westminster, Clackmannan, Clydebank and Milngavie, Colchester North, Colne Valley, Coventry North East, Crosby, Croydon Central, Croydon North East, Croydon North West, Croydon South, Cumbernauld and Kilsyth, Cunningham North, Cunningham South, Cynon Valley, Dartford, Delyn, Derby North, Derbyshire West, Devizes, Devon North, Dewsbury, Doncaster Central, Doncaster North, Dorset North, Dorset West, Dulwich, Dumbarton, Dumfries, Dundee East, Dundee West, Dunfermline East, Ealing Acton, East Kilbride, East Lothian, Eccles, Edinburgh Central, Edinburgh East, Edinburgh Leith,

Edinburgh Pentlands, Edinburgh West, Edmonton Enfield Southgate, Enfield North, Epsom and Ewell, Erewash, Erith and Crayford, Exeter, Falkirk East, Falkirk West, Fife North East, Finchley, Fulham, Fylde, Galloway and Upper Nithsdale, Gillingham, Glanford and Scunthorpe, Glasgow Cathcart, Glasgow Hillhead, Gloucester, Gordon, Great Yarmouth, Greenock and Port Glasgow, Guildford, Hamilton, Hammersmith, Hampshire East, Hastings and Rye, Havant, Hayes and Harlington, Hendon North, Henley, Hereford, Hertford and Bishops Stortford, Hertfordshire South West, Hertsmere, Hexham, Holborn and St Pancras, Holland with Boston, Hornchurch, Huddersfield, Hull City Parties, Hyndburn, Ilford North, Ilford South, Islington North, Islwyn, Kent Mid, Kilmarnock and Loudon, Kingston upon Thames, Kingswood, Kirkcaldy, Lancashire West, Lancaster, Leeds City Labour Party, Leicester City Labour Parties, Lewes, Littleborough and Saddleworth, Liverpool Garston, Liverpool Riverside, Liverpool West Derby, Livingston, Maidstone, Manchester Gorton, Mansfield, Medway, Milton Keynes, Mitcham and Morden, Mole Valley, Monklands West, Monmouth, Montgomery, Moray, Morecambe and Lunesdale, Motherwell North, Newark, Newbury, Newcastle-upon-Tyne East, Newport East, Newport West, Norfolk North, Norfolk North West, Norfolk South, Norfolk South West, Norwich City Labour Party, Nottingham South, Nuneaton, Old Bexley and Sidcup, Oldham West, Oxford West and Abingdon, Pendle, Perth and Kinross, Peterborough, Plymouth Devonport, Plymouth Drake, Plymouth Sutton, Poole, Reading East, Reading West, Reigate, Renfrew and Inverclyde, Ribble Valley, Richmond and Barnes, Romford, Romsey and Waterside, Ross Cromarty and Skye, Roxburgh and Berwickshire, Saffron Walden, St Albans, St Ives, Salisbury, Sevenoaks, Sheffield City Labour Party, Shipley, Shrewsbury and Atcham, Skipton and Ripon, Solihull, Southampton Test, Southend East, Southend West, Southport, Spelthorne, Staffordshire Mid,

Stalybridge and Hyde, Stevenage, Stirling, Stoke on Trent City Labour Parties, Strathkelvin and Bearsden, Stroud, Suffolk Central, Suffolk Coastal, Sunderland North, Surrey East, Surrey South West, Sutton and Cheam, Sutton Coldfield, Swindon, Taunton, Tayside North, Thanet South, Tonbridge and Malling, Torfaen, Tunbridge Wells, Tweeddale Ettrick and Lauderdale, Upminster, Wakefield, Wallsend, Wanstead and Woodford, Warwick and Leamington, Watford, Waveney, Wells, Westminster North, Westmorland and Lonsdale, Woking, Wolverhampton North East, Worcester, Worcestershire South, Workington, Worsley, Worthing, Wrekin, Wycombe, Wyre, and York.

Above all, I value the constant support and encouragement of the Linlithgow, formerly West Lothian, Constituency Labour Party, in my endeavours to expose the truth about this Prime Minister's actions. At each monthly meeting I report to members of the Constituency Party, and they in turn have rewarded me with their concerned interest, and repeatedly defended me in public and in private. A controversial MP is greatly fortunate to have such friends.

Acknowledgements

I would like to thank my wife Kathleen, without whom *Misrule* would not have been written, and my son Gordon and daughter Moira for their helpfulness.

The most useful kind of friend a campaigning politician can have is one who combines both knowledge of a subject and a lack of inhibition about telling the politician that he is wrong, or could be wrong, or is going off at a tangent. I record my thanks to the following candid friends for their conversation on one or more aspects of the many complex points raised in *Misrule*: Ian Aitken, Martin Alder, Lord Allen of Abbeydale, Mike Ambrose, Lord Annan, Godfrey Barker, Anthony Bevins, Rodney Bickerstaffe, Professor Robert Black, Chris Blackhurst, Christoph Bluth, Professor Anthony Bradley, Lord Brimelow, Colin Brown, Lord Bruce of Donnington, Sir Alastair Burnett, Professor Sir John Burnett, the late James Cameron, Duncan Campbell, John Carvel, Lee Chadwick, Pat Chalmers, Eric Clarke, Nick Comfort, Sir Frank Cooper, Ronnie Cramond, Sir Charles Cunningham, Malcolm Dando, Nick Davies, Jim Devine, the late Charles Douglas Home, Martin Dowle, Lord Elwyn Jones, Fred Emery, Professor John Erickson, Des Fahy, Dick Fifield, Paul Foot, Professor Sir Christopher Foster, Simon Freeman, David Frost, Arthur Gavshon, Bill Gilbey, Lord Glenamara, Diana Gould, Peter Grose, Joe Haines, Robert Harris, Lord Hatch, Julian Haviland, Peter Heathfield, Steve Hewlett, Nicholas Hyman, David Johnstone, Sir Trevor Lloyd-Hughes, the late Lord Kaldor, Michael Kenward, John Lewis, Adrian Liddell Hart, Sir Donald Maitland, Willie Makin, Marsh Marshall, Professor Sir Ronald Mason FRS, Robert Maxwell, Michael McGahey, Tom McMullan, Alan Meale, Professor Karl Miller, Alec

Moffatt, Professor Sir Nevill Mott FRS, Chris Moncrieff, Chris Mullen, Chris Mullinger, Peter Murphy, James Naughtie, Gerry Northam, Richard Norton-Taylor, Robin Oakley, John Osmond, Geoffrey Parkhouse, Barry Penrose, Clive Ponting, Stewart Prebble, Adam Raphael, Brian Raymond, John Rentoul, Peter Riddell, Dennis Ridgeway, Dr Paul Rogers, Chris Roper, George Rosie, Sir Steven Runciman, Alan Rusbridger, Tom Sawyer, Arthur Scargill, Lord Scarman, Mark Schreiber, Lord Shackleton, Lord Sherfield, Graham Smith, Maurice Smith, Peter Spencer, Sue Tinson, Stuart Trotter, Paul Walton, Jack Warden, the late David Watt, Philip Webster, Philip Whitehead, Lord Wheatley, David Wickham, Andrew Wilson, Lord Wilson of Rievaulx, Brian Wilson, Simon Winchester, Cecil Woolf, Jean Woolf, and Hugo Young.

I would also like to record my gratitude to many of my forbearing Parliamentary colleagues, mostly but not exclusively of the Labour Party, whom it would be invidious to name, and some of whom would be horrified to be named.

It would be equally invidious to name the staff of the Library of the House of Commons, who have expeditiously answered queries, as they do for any MP, and certain scholars, senior members of the Library, who have been objectively helpful on recondite issues. I am also in no doubt that I owe a debt of gratitude to a succession of exceedingly clever Clerks of the Commons, sceptical of any executive, serving in the Table Office which vets Parliamentary Questions and helps Members formulate what they want to ask.

Finally, I would like to acknowledge the drive and hard work, literary skills and sense of relevance, and friendship towards me of Julian Evans, commissioning editor of Hamish Hamilton.

Introduction

This book is not about the policies of three Conservative Governments. Once again, for better or for worse, a sufficient minority of the voting electorate – two-fifths – has plumped for Mrs Thatcher and a drift to the Right. History, and other commentators, can judge her lasting contribution, or lack of one, to the life of the nation. I am concerned here with a phenomenon much wider than the success of the Conservative Party under Mrs Thatcher, and more insidious too.

What this book is about is the personal behaviour on public matters of one particular Party leader and Prime Minister. It is about her truthfulness to people, press and Parliament. And for being 'personal' in this matter I offer no apology. Never in recent times has the highest level of British Government been run on such a personal basis.

From Walter Bagehot to the late Professor John Mackintosh, scholars have traced the increase in Prime Ministerial power. Yet from her entry into Downing Street in May 1979 up until the spring of 1982 Mrs Thatcher behaved not very differently from her immediate predecessors. Harold Macmillan once tersely observed, when asked what had influenced the course of his Government, his style and his policies, 'Events, dear boy, events!' And in the same way, it was a single event which brought about the sea-change that resulted in Mrs Thatcher's grip over government in Britain: the Falklands War.

The question of how she established such a personal and exclusive style in the spring of 1982, and how she has got away with it since, is an instructive one to examine. An omnibus reply would involve a lengthy treatise on the nature of modern government in Britain. Two circumstances provide part of the answer. The first, ironically enough, relates to the injection of an element of democracy into the selection of Conservative leader. The second relates to a trap into which the Labour Opposition has slipped.

Let me embark on the argument about democracy in the choice of a Conservative leader with an illuminating (and faithfully reported) anecdote, which occurred in the months after the Westland affair.[1]

I had an adjournment debate in April 1986[2] which I found the following week to have been quite extraordinarily widely read by leading figures of the Conservative Party. MPs do not normally bother to read another MP's end-of-day half-hour debate. But the subject of this particular debate was the role of the Prime Minister's Press Secretary, and related rather directly to the interpretation of his role by Mr Bernard Ingham, of whom much more anon in these pages.

Bumping into, as one does in the Commons, a senior Conservative Privy Councillor with whom I had been on friendly terms as a Parliamentary colleague for a quarter of a century, I had the ensuing *sotto voce* exchange:

'Read your little debate, Tam. Very interesting. You are stirring it up, aren't you!' (said with that inflection of approval, and grunt, that is a sort of Morse code between political opponents who know they oughtn't to be too disloyal, or wholly indiscreet).

'I'm just a simple, old-fashioned type,' I responded, 'who objects to the House of Commons being lied to over Law Officers' letters, by Ministers or Prime Ministers, however high and mighty. And, emphatically, I do not think that the Prime Minister's press secretary should have more say in important decisions than her Cabinet colleagues. Was I wrong in saying that Mr Ingham was the most powerful man in the British Government?'

---

[1] See Chapter 2.
[2] Adjournment debates, held every day the Commons sits, are initiated by MPs lucky in the Speaker's weekly ballot.

'Good Lord, no. You weren't wrong. But what do you want to happen? A General Election?'

'No, that's not what I am asking for. Just a change in the leadership of one of the great Parties of this country.'

'Not easily done, nowadays, m'boy.'

'What do you mean? In the days of the Magic Circle you would have done it.'

'Tam, the Magic Circle had one hell of a lot to be said for it. But, in these democratic days,' he sighed, 'it's so difficult . . .' and wandered off down the stairs, towards the Members' Cloakroom.

If we still lived in the era when the Marquis of Salisbury could assemble six grandees of the Conservative Party willing to go along, tap a Prime Minister on the shoulder, and say, 'Your time is up', in my view Mrs Thatcher would no longer be Prime Minister. Such a troupe might well have attended on her just before the Falklands War, when she was lower in the opinion polls than a Prime Minister has been since polling began. And without question she would have been winkled out of Downing Street in the aftermath of the leaking of the Solicitor General's letter during the Westland affair.

These days, a Conservative leader in Downing Street is all but impregnable, unless caught red-handed on the floor of the Commons. But the opportunity for doing just that with Mrs Thatcher was missed too, during the Westland debate. Had Neil Kinnock contented himself with quietly asking half a dozen pointed factual questions, instead of mounting a diatribe that had the effect of uniting Conservatives behind their leader, she might, in her own words quoted in the *Sunday Times*, 'not have been Prime Minister by 6 p.m. that night'. If one leader is assaulted by another leader, head-on in the House of Commons, tribal loyalties take over.

To remove a leader other than in exceptional circumstances, there has to be an election. This takes time. Bargains have to be struck. Would-be contenders and their followers are suspicious of one another. They do not act in cohesion. Mrs Thatcher has been able to pick off her critics one by one, partly because, concerned about who was to succeed, they would not form a phalanx one with another. During the grinding of the leadership electoral process, the disaffected would be identified – and suitably punished. So few of the requisite weight are prepared even to try to 'bell the cat'.

Furthermore, the nature of the Conservative selectorate has altered. When I first became an MP in 1962, the Conservative backbenches were populated by many knights of the shire and businessmen with their own interests and affairs to attend to. They liked being Members of Parliament, but their whole beings were not directed towards becoming Ministers. Times have changed. Twenty-five years later, the Conservative backbenches have a high proportion of aspirants to Ministerial office and a number of MPs who won unexpectedly both in 1983 and 1987, who now wish to be considered sufficiently loyal to be put up for safer seats in the future. The modern Conservative MP who steps out of line will find that Prime Ministerial displeasure and that of the Government Whips is conveyed to his or her Constituency Conservative Association. Difficulties more dire, if less publicised, than those in the Labour Party could arise for those who carry discontent too far. Letters to chairpersons of Constituency Associations are dreaded by those whose social position and livelihood may depend more and more on being an MP.

De facto, Mrs Thatcher has stronger reins of patronage than the British political system has witnessed since that eighteenth-century Duke of Newcastle so vividly described by Sir Lewis Namier and Bernard Pares as 'the font of preferment'. And it is this very strength of her Party position which has enabled her to cut corners, with the exercise of government and with the truth.

Yet it is not only the changing nature of her own Party in Parliament that has enabled Mrs Thatcher to get away with so much. A change in Parliamentary custom, appearing at first sight to be mechanical and of little interest to those who are not connoisseurs of Commons procedure, has come to her aid. This is the 'open question'.

In the 1960s, as in previous decades, the only questions which stuck on the Order Paper to a Prime Minister were those that pertained to the special responsibilities or public actions of the Prime Minister. Any matter that pertained more properly to the responsibilities of a departmental Minister was promptly transferred to that Minister. And quite rightly, too.

The rot began, sad to say, with Harold Wilson, who would insist in showing off in the Commons how much he knew about every facet of government. After 1970 Ted Heath, to be fair, tried to be more discriminating in answering on Prime Ministerial responsibilities, and refrained from commenting on issues which belonged more appropriately to other Cabinet Ministers. Then, in 1974, though a better Prime Minister than he had been in 1968–70, Harold Wilson reverted to his bad habit of being the universal expert on Tuesday and Thursday at 3.15 for a quarter of an hour – or more, on the arbitrary judgment of the then Mr Speakers King and Selwyn Lloyd. Jim Callaghan inherited a wider interpretation of Prime Minister's Question Time, and felt more comfortable with generalities than specific issues.

Now the Commons Order Paper for the Prime Minister consists almost exclusively of identical questions about her day's engagements,[1] and the inevitable supplementary question, 'During the course of her busy day will the Prime Minister consider, X. Y or Z?' X, Y or Z usually follows on the heels of the morning papers' headlines, and is more related to the publicity requirements of the questioner than any serious scrutiny of the Prime Minister's actions. This creates the conditions for yah-boo politics and turns

---

[1] All questions, specific and substantial, open and 'day's engagements', go into a random raffle after 4 p.m., 10 Parliamentary days (i.e. a fortnight) before they are due to be asked.

the House of Commons into what any reasonable person listening to the exchanges would call a bear-garden.

The less important result is the example set in manners to the nation – the House of Commons has always been a fairly boisterous place at the wind-up of debates. The more important result is that coherent scrutiny of the behaviour of the head of government becomes impossible. On the 'open question' MPs can do nothing other than grass-hopper from one topic to another. In the days when Prime Ministers accepted only closed questions, there was some possibility of pressing them to explain themselves to Parlia-ment and people. And this was not only because the questions were narrow and specific. Inevitably, I suppose, if questions are geared to political-point scoring at its most naked, there will be cheering and counter-cheering, snarling and counter-snarling, farmyard noises and blow-by-blow commentary from incontinent 'Parliamentarians' who develop verbal diarrhoea every Tuesday and every Thursday at 3.15 p.m. The result of this is that it is virtually impossible to hear what the Prime Minister says and latch on to those answers that are clearly inadequate. From being what the textbooks have claimed is one of the glories of British democracy, Prime Minister's Questions has de-teriorated into farce as an exercise in monitoring a Prime Minister's actions.

The position has been made worse by the recent habit, inaugurated by Michael Foot and continued by Neil Kinnock, of a twice-weekly passage of arms between Prime Minister and Opposition Leader. Let me be com-pletely candid. From my experience of him in the difficult ambience of the National Executive Committee of the Labour Party, where he performs extremely well, I have no doubt Neil Kinnock could run a Cabinet and Government. From my experience of him in political adversity over devolution together in the 1970s, I think he has guts – and has shown them on many occasions since. He is also highly principled, good at handling the Labour Party, and often an excellent platform speaker and television personality.

But I wish he would not insist on taking on the Prime Minister twice-weekly in a joust in which she has formidable briefing, has the last word by right, and is thus at an advantage.

Because I entered the Commons at twenty-nine, I am one of a comparatively small band of MPs who remember Hugh Gaitskell leading from the Opposition Front Bench. As a matter of course, if appropriate, Harold Wilson as Shadow Chancellor might question Harold Macmillan on economic matters, George Brown might question him on defence matters, or Patrick Gordon Walker if the substance of the question related to foreign affairs. If the Leader of the Opposition intervened at all, it was a newsworthy matter of weight. In his marvellous period as the Leader of the Opposition, 1963–64, Harold Wilson too was discriminating. You could hear a pin drop. And this was infinitely more dangerous for vulnerable Prime Ministers than the contemporary hullaballoo, which gives them the easiest of rides. Rational scrutiny of Prime Ministerial behaviour was actually possible.

One of my deepest political beliefs is that generalities and slogans, if ephemerally effective on the hustings, simply do not cut ice in the House of Commons. The circumstances of my political apprenticeship in Parliament, and my personal life, have caused me to worship at the shrine of fact.

Within six months of my being elected, Harold Wilson, then chairman of the Public Accounts Committee, had given me a place on the PAC. This involved four hours a week interviewing the Permanent Secretaries in their capacity as Accounting Officers. As soon as he saw that I was taking a serious interest, Sir Edmund Compton, then Comptroller and Auditor General, later to be the first Ombudsman, went out of his way to educate me in asking the right questions of very clever men (and women – for Dame Mary Smieton at Education and Dame Evelyn Sharp at Housing were among the major figures in Whitehall of the day).

It was my membership of the PAC that gave birth to the first of the parliamentary 'campaigns' in which I have been involved. I represented at that time, and for the next twenty years, part of the New Town of Livingston. A small firm of contractors, Pert's of Montrose, had been given a large slice of the new building work on the New Town, and had got into difficulties before going bankrupt. A constituent came to my surgery and asked me how it had come about that a small firm from north of the Tay had landed a huge contract south of the Forth, and insinuated that there could have been jiggery-pokery. Would I ask a Parliamentary Question? I did. The reply was a fob-off. So I took it into my head that I would pursue the matter via the Public Accounts Committee, and went along to my friend Sir Edmund, for advice as to how to do it, and to the chairman, Douglas Houghton by that time (now Lord Houghton of Sowerby). They were both helpful. Being asked a Parliamentary Question by a novice MP was routine and of little consequence. Being arraigned before the Public Accounts Committee, 100 years old, and before the Commons had spawned Select Committees, was quite another matter. The Permanent Secretary of the Scottish Office, no less, had to get himself massively briefed. In this then rather secluded backwater, the mandarins were not used to this kind of assault. Even when the report proved that I was justified, a lot of senior persons (among them a somewhat aghast Labour Group of Scottish MPs) were not best pleased. But it taught me a lesson. Never be fobbed off with an inadequate answer.

I learned something else from Sir Edmund Compton, too, which was never to go into a campaign without informed and interested friends and, crucially, friends of a stature to tell me if they thought I was wrong or on a wild goose chase. This is the weakness of having, or relying on, research assistants. They are quite happy to egg their MP employers on, and usually have neither the authority nor the knowledge to press a red warning light. Too often I have seen research assistants encourage their MPs on irresponsible courses of action. It was Sir Edmund Compton who told me bluntly that I was on shaky ground if I proposed to attack Sir Thomas Padmore, then Permanent Secretary at the Department of Transport on railway matters; I beat a quick retreat, and rightly in retrospect, though my interest in railways is unabated, and I am sponsored by the National Union of Railwaymen as one of their MPs. But Sir Edmund did give me the green light on nagging John Boyd-Carpenter, chairman of the PAC after a change of Government in 1964, into hauling Sebastian Ziani de Ferranti and his senior managers before the PAC over the question of the Bloodhound missile. The result was a finding on excess profits, and the repayment of millions of pounds to the Exchequer.

My next campaign was to save the country money too, a great deal as it turned out. It started when I happened to be watching television news during one Christmas Recess and saw pictures of Defence Secretary Denis Healey going through Paris with motorcycle outriders in white gloves. I then saw him appear on the screen to claim that he had signed an agreement for the Anglo-French Variable Geometry aircraft, 'the most advanced fighter aircraft in the world'. I knew this was simply not right. By that time, F1-11s were certainly winging their way over Edwards Air Force Base – much more advanced aircraft than AFVGs – and it was preposterous for Denis to say any such thing. From that episode, I learned something that has been with me for twenty years and more. Apparently small Ministerial inexactitudes are part of larger Ministerial inexactitudes, small inconsistencies tend to be part of larger inconsistencies, and eventually small Prime Ministerial lies tend to be part of larger Prime Ministerial lies.

A battery of Parliamentary Questions exposed the AFVG for what it was, an expensive nonsense which would have been out of date as soon as it was off the production line. Getting the agreement scrutinised and cancelled a year or two before it would have been cancelled anyway saved many millions of taxpayers' money.

My main motives in campaigning over Aldabra Atol in 1967 were no less monetary than ideological. I had been opposed to the Labour Government's East of Suez policy ever since I went to the Borneo War in 1965, and I was genuinely concerned about the ecosystem of a unique Indian Ocean atoll that provided a home for the flightless rail, the pink-footed booby and the giant tortoise, among others. The idea of an RAF staging post for supplying a Far East commitment in which I did not believe, and which would bring rats and other vermin to destroy the ecosystem of Aldabra, appalled me. But, as in the case of the AFVG, it was a seemingly small technical and factual error that was to get the campaign on the road. The Ministry of Public Buildings and Works told me in a Parliamentary Answer that the in-filling for the runway would be mined on the atoll itself. Apart from the appalling damage to the mangrove and other vegetation, this seemed to me not to add up. I happened to know about the nature of coral limestone. It is hard and brittle on the extreme surface. A few inches underneath it is soft and chunky and utterly unsuitable for in-filling, let alone as a basis for carrying heavy long-distance transport planes on a runway. I then plagued the Minister, Bob Mellish, with questions about the cost of transporting many thousands of tons of rock from East Africa. At the same time, I sent copies of my seventy Parliamentary Questions to vice-President Hubert Humphrey, whom I knew; to crusty old Senator McLellan of Arkansas, Chairman of the Senate Appropriations Committee; Congressman Henry Reuss; Glenn Seaborg, Chairman of the US Atomic Energy Authority; Ed Wenk, Secretary of the Marine Sciences Council; and Bill Carey, head of the Science Section of the Bureau of the Budget, at whose house my wife and I had stayed for ten days in Washington, while I visited these and other leading Americans. One and all sent my letter and questions to Secretary of Defense Macnamara, asking for a comment.

To his consternation, Denis Healey was confronted with all this unease about his Aldabra plans in Washington – and was livid about what one of his backbenchers had got up to. In the meantime, I had taken the chance to pay a midnight visit at his hotel to Dillon Ripley, the long-serving Secretary of the Smithsonian, who happened to be passing through London and who has constitutional access, as of right, to the President of the United States. Ripley undertook to raise Aldabra with Lyndon Johnson as a matter of urgency. He kept his word. Within days, Harold Wilson had announced to a mostly amused and approving House of Commons and Parliamentary Labour Party, but to a glum Labour Party Front Bench, the cancellation of the staging post at Aldabra Atoll.

If I make reference to my history as a thorn in the flesh of certain Labour Ministers, it is to suggest that any attack I make on Mrs Thatcher is not simply a routine matter of attacking political opponents. The House of Commons is a place for diversity, and heaven help the country if there were 630 MPs all like me – or like any other MP, one hopes. But there is a place for the scrutiniser – and a scrutiniser I have always tried to be. One of the differences between Labour Ministers and the current Prime Minister is that if they concluded that they might ultimately be wrong, they admitted it with good grace. Mrs Thatcher refuses to admit she could be wrong, and brazens it out. Moreover, the worst that could be said about Labour Ministers was that they were open to criticism in their assessments, of AFVG and Aldabra among other issues. They were never suspected of deliberately lying to the House of Commons.

Having created what the late Cabinet Minister Tony Greenwood, half-pleased, called a 'trail of mayhem' for the Labour Government, I came a cropper. As a Member of the Select Committee on Science and Technology, I visited Porton Down. Campaigning against chemical and

biological weapons, I talked very freely to Lawrence Marks
of the *Observer*, and then, as a Division Bell rang, handed
him the transcript of the Committee proceedings – which
I genuinely thought had been published. They had not.
The Ministry of Defence (as I now know) put the late Sir
Harry Legge Bourke up to complaining about the leak as
a matter of privilege. I owned up straight away. And was,
on 24 July 1968, the last MP ever to be hauled to the Bar
of the House, to be reprimanded by the Speaker, donning
his black hat. Mr Speaker King loved it. *Schadenfreude*
abounded. James Callaghan, to his credit, said he did not
vote in blood rituals. Tony Benn locked himself in the
toilet. Michael Foot spoke for me. But I was rebuked by
vote of the House, after being interrogated by the Privi-
leges Committee, led by Elwyn Jones, Attorney General,
ex-Nuremberg prosecutor.

Anybody who says that an MP can shrug off such an
experience and not care cannot know what it is like. It was
hell. But it did develop an even thicker skin than I already
had. And by the late 1960s that skin was already a pretty
thick hide.

First and above all, for twenty-four years I have been
most happily married to the same woman. Kathleen has
been marvellous and loyal, but she has a critical mind of
her own, and frequently asks me to justify myself, my
views and actions, to her. To her family I am close: for over
thirty years, my father-in-law John Wheatley, a former
Labour MP and Law Officer, sat in the Court of Session
in the High Court and Court of Appeal in Scotland, and
he often asks me the kind of searching questions to which
there ought to be an answer.

But it has also been my good fortune to have been
involved as a young MP with a variety of formidable
operators. Within weeks of being at Westminster, I was
working for Dick Crossman, whose Parliamentary Private
Secretary I was to be from 1964 to 1970, and with whom
I was to stay, while in London, at 9 Vincent Square until
he died. Diarist and great political inquisitor that my boss

was, he taught me to ensure I had a good case. More formidable still, in a way, was the man to whom Dick Crossman told me to work in my capacity as Secretary of the Labour Party Standing Conference on the Sciences from 1963 to 1965: Patrick Blackett, sub-lieutenant on HMS *Barham* at Jutland, Nobel Prize Winner in Physics, Rector of Imperial College, President-to-be of the Royal Society, did not suffer fools gladly. Nor did my Cambridge tutors with whom I always kept in contact, Christopher Morris and Noel Annan, Professor Joan Robinson and Professor Harry Johnson (later to go off to Chicago as Milton Friedman's colleague). To Nicky Kaldor, with whom I kept in touch until he died, I poured out my constituency economic problems, which he said resulted in the Regional Employment Premium – a useful and beneficial measure in its day.

I worked, too, with Dr Vivian Bowden, then the wonderfully and convincingly imaginative Principal of the Manchester College of Science and Technology (later created Lord Bowden of Chesterfield), one of the architects of the 'White Heat of the Technological Revolution' – a concept not to be sneered at, which gave hope to manufacturing industry in Britain. I was the politician on the Labour Party Science Delegation to Russia in March 1964, along with Dr David Shoenberg FRS, Director of the Mond Low-Temperature Laboratory in Cambridge, Professor Colin Adamson, the distinguished electrical engineer, and Tony Bradshaw, Professor of Metallurgy at Imperial College, London. I say this not to name-drop but to explain that I look at political leaders from a rather different, perhaps more searching perspective, than many colleagues whose whole being is in politics.

If the 1960s were spent working for the white heat of the technological revolution, and in particular for R. H. S. Crossman as Minister of Housing, Leader of the House of Commons, and Secretary of State for Health and Social Security, the 1970s were spent on devolution and Scottish nationalism.

But a crucial point came for me one day in 1965, when I was invited to lunch by the then President of the Royal Society, Sir Howard Florey. He had with him Sir Ashley Miles, then Foreign Secretary of the Royal Society, and other heavyweights, who asked me if I would take a continuing interest in science, since few other MPs would. I promised. And for twenty-two years, during twenty of which I have been a weekly columnist for *New Scientist*, I have kept that promise. This has acted as a discipline in reminding me each week that fact is sacred.

It is this background that makes me so contemptuous of those who, to paraphrase Sir Robert Armstrong, economise with the truth.

Such is the potted political history of one of Mrs Thatcher's critics.

Contrary to belief, I have not always loathed her. I first met her when she was the late Charlie Pannell's pair. A friend of mine, MP for West Leeds, and doyen of Parliamentary procedure, he always said she was a really tough and ruthless and able operator. And then, Mrs Thatcher and I had a mutual friend, Airey Neave, outrageously murdered in the Westminster car park by we still don't know who. Out of the side of his mouth he had said to me, during the leadership election against Ted Heath, 'Put your money on the filly, Tam, if I were you.' And I did.

I, like many others, wished her well as the first woman to become a Party leader. At that point we could hardly guess what was to come.

I am accused of seizing upon any broomstick with which to beat the Prime Minister. This charge against me is wide of the mark. Not a word appears in these pages about the so-called 'Oman affair'. And it is not only because I have a distaste for involving peoples' families in any examination of their political behaviour. Though it is my impression that my Parliamentary colleagues were likely to be right, and certainly that Peter Shore and Dale Campbell-Savours were asking legitimate questions, I thought the particular case against Mrs Thatcher was possibly 'not proven', to use the Scots legal term, and therefore I uttered not a word.

I am also accused of consigning myself to the ghetto of eccentricity by saying such dreadful things about the British Prime Minister. The very real problem here is that no other Prime Minister has behaved in anything like the brazenly deceitful ways of Mrs Thatcher. And to many decent people, it is simply not credible that a British Prime Minister should act in such wicked style. There is an understandable credibility gap.

I strongly believe in political good manners. I never shout in the Commons. I never bawl. It is well known that I have been thrown out on two occasions, but those incidents can only be understood in the light of what was actually said.

On the first occasion, on 2 May 1984, I asked Norman Tebbit whether, as Secretary of State for Trade and Industry, he planned to follow up any of the initiatives of Cecil Parkinson's trade visit to Argentina of 1980, now that civilian government had been re-established there. Mr Tebbit replied that there were no initiatives outstanding. I pointed out that Mr Parkinson had congratulated the junta at the time on approaching its economic problems along the same lines as Mrs Thatcher's Government. What I then wanted to get at was that Mr Parkinson had also, on a recent *Panorama* television programme, admitted that he knew about the Peruvian peace plans which should have stopped the Falklands conflict escalating into full-scale war. Mrs Thatcher had denied all knowledge of the proposals at the time she gave the order to sink the *General Belgrano* – which, since Mr Parkinson was a member of the War Cabinet, I knew to be a nonsense. Mr Speaker and I had this exchange:

Mr Speaker: 'Order. This is a trade matter.'

Mr Dalyell: '– with the clear implication that the Prime Minister is lying –'

Mr Speaker: 'Order. The hon. Gentleman will have to withdraw that word.'

Mr Dalyell: 'By implication, it is a matter of fact, not supposition –'

Mr Speaker: 'Nevertheless, the hon. Gentleman has been here long enough to know that he should not attribute lying to any right hon. or hon. Member.'

Mr Dalyell: 'By implication, what the right hon. Gentleman –'

Mr Speaker: Order. The hon. Gentleman knows exactly what I am getting at.'

Mr Dalyell: 'The proof is here. I have the text of the Prime Minister's –'

Mr Speaker: 'Order. I say to the hon. Gentleman, who is a very experienced Member, that this takes up time out of questions and he must withdraw that word.'[1]

I refused, and I was suspended. But the harsh fact is, as we shall see in the opening chapter, that although I used 'unparliamentary language' in the House, Mrs Thatcher was indeed lying. Indeed, now even James Prior in his memoirs substantiates my account of the Prime Minister's state of knowledge of the Peruvian peace proposals.[2]

Nearly two and a half years later, on 29 October 1986 there was a repetition during the debate on Westland. There has never been any full account by the Prime Minister of exactly who ordered the leaking of the Solicitor General's letter, and I wanted to make this point forcibly in order to demonstrate that the principle of truthfulness

[1] Hansard, 2 May 1984, cols 345–6.
[2] *A Balance of Power*, Hamish Hamilton, 1986.

in the House, which is the fulcrum of our system, was being undermined. This is what happened:

> **Mr Dalyell:** 'There was no full account. To say that the Prime Minister did not take part in the leak is a sustained, brazen deception. It is straightforward dishonesty . . . The Prime Minister is a sustained, brazen deceiver now hiding cynical performances.'
>
> **Mr Deputy Speaker (Mr Harold Walker):** 'Order. The hon. Gentleman knows that he cannot say that and that he must withdraw that remark about the Prime Minister.'
>
> **Mr Dalyell:** 'I say that she is a bounder, a liar, a deceiver, a cheat and a crook.'
>
> **Mr Deputy Speaker:** 'Order. The hon. Gentleman knows perfectly well that he cannot say that. He must either withdraw his remarks or I must invoke the powers invested in me and my responsibilities to the House. I hope that the hon. Gentleman, who is a very experienced parliamentarian, will withdraw those remarks.'[1]

My refusal to comply meant that I was suspended again. The only difference between the two occasions is that on this one I have been proved right even more expeditiously. Five months afterwards, in March 1987, nine senior journalists reconstructed for *World in Action* the sequence of events in the Westland affair.[2] They were unanimous that the leaking of the letter was done solely for political purposes, to discredit Michael Heseltine, and that it was authorised by the Prime Minister. Their version was greeted with silence from Number Ten Downing Street – the silence of those who knew they had no grounds whatsoever for protest.

I have not particularly enjoyed being thrown out of the

---

[1] Hansard, 29 October 1986, col. 389.
[2] *World in Action*, broadcast 30 March 1987.

House for abusing long-standing rules of conduct which are central to the continuance of an effective Parliament. But if heeding these rules means that falsehoods flourish unchecked and a vigorous institution becomes an empty parody, what other course is open?

The seed of suspicion about Mrs Thatcher's own conduct was sown in my mind by the reason that emerged as to why she had sacked Reggie Maudling as Shadow Foreign Secretary. 'You are getting in my way,' she told him.[1]

Apart from the fact that Reggie Maudling (like Iain Macleod and Edward Boyle, Conservatives of a totally different disposition from Mrs Thatcher) was a friend of mine, I was very uneasy.

For me, Reggie Maudling, MP for Barnet, was infinitely more intelligent, more understanding of the problems outside the Home Counties, more compassionate, and more tolerant than his Parliamentary neighbour in Finchley, Margaret Thatcher. The notion that she should dismiss him because he was 'getting in her way' boded ill for Britain. She steamrollers dissent. It is a myth to suppose she likes men around her who stand up to her and argue with her. It was revealing, for example, that David Gompert, one of Alexander Haig's close advisers during the shuttle diplomacy of 1982, should say during the Thames TV programme marking the fifth anniversary of the Falklands War, that Mrs Thatcher explicitly overruled senior members of the Cabinet. And the American impression was certainly that she treated them with contempt.

Cabinet Government, as it has long been understood in Britain, has simply broken down. The Deputy Prime Minister has been shunted off to the House of Lords, pleased to be allowed by grace and favour the trappings of public life. I am frankly sad to see Willie Whitelaw, whom I first knew as Harold Macmillan's Under-Secretary at the Ministry of Labour, and Opposition Chief Whip, reduced to an awful shadow of his former self, unctuously

[1] Beryl Maudling in the *Standard*, 27 June 1985.

praising Mrs Thatcher during the occasional TV appearance. The Lord Chancellor has become a time-server of a kind that Quintin Hogg in his great days would have regarded with contempt. For Chancellor of the Exchequer Mrs Thatcher has Nigel Lawson, who neither sees himself nor is seen by others as a possible Prime Minister. As for the Foreign Secretary, there was even doubt that he would accompany her on her trip to Moscow earlier this year.

However, the Prime Minister did take her press secretary to the Soviet Union. And the commentator at Tblisi airport seemed to understand the pecking order perfectly when, against the visual image of the Prime Ministerial party descending from the aircraft in the Georgian capital, he observed, 'Mr Ingham is there, shepherding his flock.' What has become of Cabinet Government in Britain when the elected Foreign Secretary becomes part of the flock of the Prime Minister's non-elected press secretary?

The images on the screen were all too symbolic of the reality of affairs. Mrs Thatcher has the capacity to reduce Cabinet Ministers as men. She has equally shown herself able to engineer the absence of a natural successor. Peter Walker and Geoffrey Howe are growing stale in her service. Other Cabinet Ministers of her era are either cronies or yesterday's men. Probably she would wish that her eventual successor would be a man, but a man two political generations her junior.

Certainly Mrs Thatcher says that she likes to indulge in lively argument. Yet look at this claim closely. She wallows in confrontation in the House of Commons and other places. She will make a public spectacle of seeming to take on Mr Gorbachov. She can put on her fishwife act at whim, haranguing journalists and television interviewers. But does she really like arguing with clever, independent people around her? The answer is that from the day she sacked Reggie Maudling, she revealed her dislike of cleverer people than herself, arguing a case at close quarters. She does not appreciate being challenged – least of all by potential successors.

This assumption of power for her own exercise alone, and the desire to keep it at all costs, are the most predatory, authoritarian and dishonest trends in Government that Britain has ever experienced. I will not repeat my epithets of 29 October 1986. But Margaret Thatcher must be exposed for what she is. Successful or not, that is this book's paramount aim.

1

Escalating a War

If we go back six eventful years to the circumstances of the sinking of the Argentine cruiser *General Belgrano*, it is not simply because 368 sailors were drowned and the Falklands War moved from second gear to fifth gear.

It is rather because the Prime Minister who, at Chequers, before lunch on Sunday 2 May 1982, ordered the destruction of that ship, who has control over F1-11s leaving British bases to attack Tripoli and Benghazi, and has her finger on the nuclear button. Therefore, her behaviour in a crunch situation is a matter of lasting, not ephemeral importance, as long as she remains in Number Ten Downing Street.

The charges against the British Prime Minister could hardly be graver. I say she is guilty of gross deception. I say she is guilty of lying to the House of Commons – sustained, calculating lying, as became clear during the eleven days of Clive Ponting's trial at the Old Bailey.[1] And, as I said in her own North London constituency, at a public meeting organised in Finchley Town Hall by the Finchley Constituency Labour Party, she is guilty of calculated murder, not for the national interests of our country, not for the protection of our servicemen, but for her own political ends.

[1] For a full account of the trial in February 1985, read *The Right to Know* by Clive Ponting, Sphere Books: pp. 169–96.

Those who make such a charge against their head of government had better be very clear that they can substantiate it, otherwise they would be wise not to say it. Therefore, I offer the reader no apology for going into detail.

For over two years, in the face of repeated questioning, Mrs Thatcher stuck to it in the House of Commons that our submarine, HMS *Conqueror*, had detected the cruiser *General Belgrano* about 8 p.m. on Sunday 2 May 1982. This was formally endorsed in paragraph 110 of the official White Paper, *The Falkland Islands: The Lessons*. It was further endorsed in Sir John Fieldhouse's Official Report on the War – the kind of report that has been required of every Commander-in-Chief since the Crimean War.

But it was not true that HMS *Conqueror* had detected the *Belgrano* about 8 p.m. on Sunday 2 May. The truth was very significantly different.[1]

On her passive sonar, before 4 p.m. on Friday 30 April, HMS *Conqueror* had picked up, first of all an oiler,[2] and then the *Belgrano* and her escorts, the *Hipolito Bouchard* and the *Piedra Buena*. From four o'clock that South Atlantic afternoon, at periscope depth, HMS *Conqueror* had closed in on the 'Argentine Surface Group'. Throughout the forenoon of Saturday 1 May, still at periscope depth and at a distance of 4000 yards, HMS *Conqueror* monitored the *Belgrano* and escorts 'razzing' – that is, refuelling at sea. In such a position, any sailor knows that a ship is a sitting-duck target.

So this question arises. If the forty-four-year-old cruiser, survivor of Pearl Harbor,[3] was such a threat to the modern

---

[1] I thought I detected the jury at the Ponting trial gulp collectively as it became clear at the Old Bailey that this aspect of the Report had been altered behind Sir John Fieldhouse's back, without his knowledge.

[2] Refuelling vessel.

[3]. Commissioned in 1938, the *General Belgrano* had seen distinguished service throughout World War Two as USS *Phoenix*. She was sold to Peron by the United States in 1951.

ships of the British Task Force, why was an order to sink not given there and then? After all, the cruiser and oiler were at the mercy of the submarine.

No such order was given. From midday on that Saturday, 1 May, 'discreetly' as the diarist Lieutenant Mahendra Sethia, supplies officer of the *Conqueror*, put it, at a distance of 10,000 yards, the *Conqueror* followed the *Belgrano* and escorts. At 8.07 p.m. an order went out from the operational commander Vice-Admiral Walter Allara, on board the Argentine aircraft carrier, *Veinticinco de Mayo*, ordering the surface group back to Staten Island on the coast of Argentina. That order was confirmed by the naval command in Buenos Aires at 1.19 a.m. the following Sunday morning.

Both these orders, like most other orders, were intercepted by us. Or, more precisely, by the AD470 high-frequency Marconi transceiver equipment on board the Task Force. From there they were flashed back to Ascension Island, and then to GCHQ at Cheltenham, where they were decrypted in a minute to a minute and a half. This was not a very difficult task at the best of times – it was even simpler when those who had devised the orders had been trained by us at Portsmouth shortly before.

The information about the instructions to the Argentine Surface Group was corroborated, I believe, by way of Chile. Certainly, as the incident of the crashed British helicopter bears out, Chile was giving covert help.[1] And the leaked documents from the junior Foreign Office clerk, Geoffrey Dennis, make it clear that the reason why Britain

[1] The Royal Navy crew of the Sea King helicopter which crash-landed near Punta Arenas in southern Chile on 18 May 1982 'disappeared' for several days and supposedly made their way to safety under their own steam. In fact the Chilean Navy were seen to pick up at least one man. All three crew were then co-operatively treated and hurried out of the country. The helicopter was not on the complement of any task force ship, contrary to what the Ministry of Defence said, according to Duncan Campbell in the *New Statesman*, but was operating from a secret British military base inside Chile.

could not contemplate imposing sanctions on the odious regime of General Pinochet was that, had we done so, we would have jeopardised the help that we were receiving from Chile in relation to our position in the Falklands.[1]

I am absolutely certain the same information about the orders to the *Belgrano* came to London from the Americans. It was hardly in the interests of the United States that two Western, Christian nations should be fighting one another; and Washington had an interest in passing on intelligence which showed that one friend was not in fact threatening the forces of another friend. Should any reader doubt the capacity of American Intelligence to come by such information, let us recollect that the USA had a satellite in polar orbit. If the Americans had no difficulty in intercepting signals to a Russian MiG fighter, over the Sea of Okutsk, in relation to the Korean airliner 007, they would have had not the slightest problem in intercepting orders from the Argentine mainland to their ships. These were passed on, to London.

Let me pause in the narrative to insert two comments.

I am very coy about revealing sources. And never would I reveal a source, wittingly, without the express authority of that source to do so. At one level, it is a simple matter of honour: if a man is told something in confidence, and agrees to the confidence, then in honour bound he should stick to his word. At another level, shielding sources is a matter of self-interest for a politician who wishes to be effective. By relentlessly asking questions in the House of Commons, and making speeches in the country and in Parliament, an MP identifies himself or herself in the public mind as a 'receptacle for information'. If such an MP were ever to be seen to let an informant down, as, to his great

---

[1] In 1985 it became clear via documents leaked by Mr Dennis from the Overseas Development Administration that Her Majesty's Government had a contingency plan to sever ties with the Chilean junta if the political climate was not improved there. But it was said that this could carry 'unacceptable penalties' including 'co-operation we enjoy over the Falklands'.

regret, the editor of the *Guardian* let Sarah Tisdall down, then who would – or should – ever trust that MP ever again? Why should anyone put his or her career at stake by confiding in an untrustworthy MP? And yet without 'deep-throats', MPs would often find it difficult to know the right questions to ask. Later, I shall deploy the case for having a senior body to whom dissatisfied civil servants can appeal, which I helped impose on the Labour Party at the Bournemouth Conference in 1985. In the meantime, in asking the reader to believe my statements about American information, and so much else, I can only point to my track record of factual accuracy, where I have not yet once slipped on the proverbial banana skin – an event which would afford delicious pleasure to a large number of great and distinguished people.

The second interruption to the narrative must be a reference to a remarkable book, *The Sinking of the Belgrano*, by Desmond Rice and Arthur Gavshon.[1] It was Rice and Gavshon who delved into the actual orders to which I have referred. Desmond Rice was the President of the Royal Dutch Shell Company in Argentina, and thus had many contacts. He was also a friend of Arthur Gavshon, who had been my friend since 1963, when I began to work as a young MP for the late Dick Crossman, diarist and Cabinet Minister in the 1964–70 Wilson Government.[2]

I spent some hours persuading Gavshon, a journalist so senior that he regularly saw British Prime Ministers alone and had interviewed several US Presidents, that he ought to take an interest in the *Belgrano*. What eventually caught

[1] Secker & Warburg, 1984.

[2] One of my first instructions from Crossman after he entered the Ministry of Housing, the empire of the late Dame Evelyn Sharp, was: 'Whatever Evelyn and George Moseley [then Principal Private Secretary] make me do, you make sure that if Arthur Gavshon wants to see me, he is slotted in.' Crossman was ever concerned with his image in the USA and Europe, and Gavshon was Diplomatic Correspondent for Europe of the American Associated Press.

his interest was that never, in thirty years' experience, had he known so many mutually inconsistent explanations from any British Government. As in the case of the intercepted Argentine signals and the supposed time of sighting of the *Belgrano* by HMS *Conqueror*, small inconsistencies led to larger inconsistencies, small economies with the truth to larger economies with the truth, small lies to ever larger lies.

Let us return to the narrative. Why, knowing what she did about the directions and movements of the *Belgrano*, and the orders under which it was proceeding, did the British Prime Minister sanction the first ever action by a nuclear-powered submarine in anger? She must have known that in those waters, at that time of year, it was more likely that 1000 men would be drowned than the 368 who actually perished?

It is no good blaming the Navy professionals. Before Admiral of the Fleet Lord Lewin left operational headquarters at Northwood that Sunday morning for Chequers, the consensus of opinion was that it would be more dangerous to attack the old cruiser than not to do so. This was surely a correct professional judgment, since predictably, and predicted, the real threat did not come from the 6-inch guns, range thirteen miles, of the *Belgrano*, but from land-based aircraft with their traditional menace to capital ships.[1] Rear Admiral Sandy Woodward, in charge of the task force, became known as 'Burma Star' Woodward because he correctly kept his aircraft carriers so far to the east – as far out of range of mainland Argentina as possible.

---

[1] On 21 April I had been to see Mrs Thatcher in her room at the Commons, in the presence of Ian Gow MP. I opened the meeting by saying that one of my earliest childhood memories had been the distress of my mother when she heard that the *Prince of Wales* and the *Repulse* had been sunk off Malaya, and that the Falklands conflict was all about the same thing: land-based aircraft and capital ships. She replied that one of her chief advisers was Admiral Sir Henry Leach, who was the son of the captain of the *Prince of Wales*, and that she could not be more conscious of the danger.

The consequence of attacking the *Belgrano* was seen to be that airborne retaliation would swiftly follow. It did.

I believe – no *Belgrano*, no *Sheffield*, no *Ardent*, no *Antelope*, no *Atlantic Conveyor*, no *Coventry*, no Goose Green, no Bluff Cove. Be that as it may, the sinking of the *Belgrano* was not the plan of Naval Command at Northwood.

Why then did Mrs Thatcher, together with Lord Lewin, do it?

Because she knew something else that Saturday evening, 1 May, and that Sunday morning.

The something else was that the Government of Peru, backed by the United States, was putting forward peace proposals that the Americans, the United Nations, the Organisation of American States, our European partners, and many others would have expected her to accept. But, had the Prime Minister accepted them, she knew that she would be deprived of the 'military victory' which is what the Falklands War was all about from an early stage.

Such a charge levelled against a British Prime Minister in a situation of undeclared war may seem horrendous. It implies cold, callous calculation. So it is necessary to be very clear. The charge is not that Mrs Thatcher manipulated Galtieri into a military adventure against the Falklands. It is that, given the knowledge of a likely attack on the Falklands, the Prime Minister was quite content to let the situation run and, by seeming inaction, to lure the Argentines on to the punch. A little war, deemed to be righteous by public opinion, might restore the domestic political fortunes of a Prime Minister who sat lower in the opinion polls than any Prime Minister had done since political polling began.

If such a scenario appears far-fetched, consider the facts. Paragraphs 146 to 156 of the Franks Committee (to which the author gave evidence) show how our excellent ambassador in Buenos Aires, Anthony Williams, was giving warnings to London on 3 March 1982 about likely attacks on the Falklands. On 7 March, in her own handwriting,

Franks records, the Prime Minister was noting that we must 'have contingency plans'. Now someone who asks for contingency plans at the beginning of March cannot have it, as she said to me in the House of Commons during Prime Minister's Questions six months later,[1] that the Falklands War came out of the blue on Wednesday 31 March. No, it did not.

Besides, the truth is often blurted out in anger. During the momentous debate of 3 April 1982 – the first Saturday morning on which the Commons had sat since Suez a quarter of a century before – John Nott, the Defence Secretary, was interrupted by Julian Amery in hostile manner. Why were we unprepared? The sharp-tongued Defence Secretary snapped back that we were not unprepared, preparations had been going on for weeks. And so they had.

On 1/2 May, had the Peruvian proposals been accepted, or even properly considered, it would have looked like a fudge and compromise – the momentum would have been lost, and public opinion would have begun to ask what had led up to such a situation, and whether the despatch of the battle fleet was really a justified response in the late twentieth century. After all, one of the key conditions for the 'just war', as laid down by St Augustine and St Thomas Aquinas, is that everything possible should be done to avoid war before it starts. It is a condition most emphatically unfulfilled in the case of the Falklands.

It has been Mrs Thatcher's line, and that of her loyal colleagues, to play down the Peruvian proposals to the point of dismissal – to suggest that they never amounted to anything, and that in any case she did not know about them until after the *Belgrano* was sunk. This is a travesty of the truth.

Along with Dr Guillermo Makin, of Girton College, Cambridge, I went on a four-day visit to Lima (paid for by me) to ascertain what had really happened. In his study

[1] 26 October 1982.

in the Presidential Palace in Lima, President Belaúnde Terry explained what had taken place. His plan was, basically, to have Peruvian and American troops temporarily on the Falklands; for the Argentine forces to withdraw; and for the British Task Force to turn round and go back to Ascension. However, Belaúnde told me that the Americans were not by this stage acceptable to the Argentines, and the Peruvians were not acceptable to the British. So he then proposed to have Mexican, West German, and Canadian troops. He knew, the President said, that our Ambassador, our Government, and our Prime Minister knew what the Peruvians were doing.[1] Besides, since the Peruvian peace proposals were on the international press tapes, it would have been very odd if the British Government had not known.

Later I sat in the home of Dr Manuel Ulloa, Prime Minister of Peru in 1982 and Chairman of the Development Committee of the World Bank, in the Mira Flores district of Lima. What did we take the Peruvians for? 'We were negotiators.' Negotiators had to be in touch with both sides. 'I know that through Lord Hugh Thomas and other channels, your Government and your Prime Minister knew exactly what we were trying to do. Negotiators have to be in touch with both parties!' said Dr Ulloa.

Oscar Maourtua, head of Belaúnde's office, had spent two years as a graduate student of Pembroke College, Oxford. This able young official explained to me that the whole Government machine in Peru had come to a halt that weekend, so concerned were they at what was happening – not least that a European power, which had signed Protocol One of the non-nuclear Treaty of Tlatelolco,[2] was bringing nuclear weapons to South American waters, where no nuclear weapons had ever been before. And so

---

[1] The President was particularly friendly with the British Ambassador, whose wife was Spanish, and whose family had been kind in Spain to the Belaúndes during the first military government of Peru.

[2] The Treaty of Tlatelolco, signed in 1967 by the countries of South America, bound participants to keep nuclear weapons out of the area.

we were. 'I know,' said Maourtua, 'that your Government
and your Prime Minister knew what Peru was trying to do
that Sunday morning.[1,2]

Distancing herself from that which it is embarrassing to
know, and denying all knowledge of awkward truths, has
become part of the hallmark of Mrs Thatcher's Government, as we shall find again during the saga of the Solicitor
General's letter during the Westland affair, and after the
raid on the BBC in Glasgow.

I have no doubt whatever that I was told the truth in
Lima. If the reader asks why Peru did not raise complaint
and produce documentary evidence, the response is understandable. They were a right-wing government. They
were faced with debt problems, and still more problems
from the Sendero Luminoso guerrillas. They had no wish
to become embroiled in British domestic politics with
no advantage, and possibly considerable disadvantage, to
themselves in relation to European and American banks.
By 1984, and the period in which the Select Committee on
Foreign Affairs was incubating its questions on the events
of 1–2 May, events in Peru had moved on. But we do not
have to depend on Peruvian evidence.

We can turn to the United States, and the memoirs of
Alexander Haig, Mrs Thatcher's fervent admirer. In his
book *Caveat*[3] the former NATO Commander and American Secretary of State writes the revealing words, 'Nevertheless he [Belaúnde] gained acceptance in principle from

[1] Later the public testimony of Dr Arias Stella, Foreign Minister of
Peru, in a position to know at first hand, on *Panorama* to Mr Fred Emery,
was to endorse exactly what had been said to me in Lima.

[2] And there was another peace initiative too, which the Prime Minister
discarded. At the instigation of the Mexican president, José Portillo, and
through the mediation of Edward Du Cann, a Mexican Minister went to
Downing Street in late April to tell Mrs Thatcher that General Galtieri
had telephoned his President. Galtieri was willing to negotiate a withdrawal if Mrs Thatcher would travel to Mexico. She did nothing.

[3] Weidenfeld & Nicolson, 1984; p. 293.

both parties . . .' Some corrections were made after the book went to press, as is clear from the erratum slip in the beginning of the book. But this statement was not altered, and it is crucial. Further, this assessment has been supported by Woody Goldberg, Haig's assistant; Dean Fisher, the Assistant Secretary for Public Affairs; the official spokesman of the State Department at the time; and other leading Americans in a position to know. Why on earth should Haig think that there was agreement in principle if one side, the British, did not even *know* about the negotiations? The Americans are quite clear that Mrs Thatcher – who had not called together her full Cabinet to discuss the conduct of the Falklands War between 2 April and 5 May, after HMS *Sheffield* had been sunk – did indeed know.

To those who ask whether the Prime Minister was not taking an enormous risk by spurning Peruvian/American peace proposals, the answer is that it was indeed reckless. But then Mrs Thatcher is a gambler with fortune, and I suppose, had she not been so, she would not have challenged Edward Heath, when others flinched from doing so, and become Leader of the Conservative Party. Maybe she had no real notion of the colossal potential for disaster for the Task Force?

But it is not only evidence from abroad that belies Mrs Thatcher's claim for ignorance of the Peruvian proposals. Pressed by Fred Emery on *Panorama*, Cecil Parkinson let the cat out of the bag. Yes, said Parkinson, we (he was a member of the War Cabinet) knew all about the peace proposals that Sunday morning, 'primarily those of President Belaúnde'. And pressed by me on the BBC *Brasstacks* programme, Cranley Onslow, then Minister of State at the Foreign Office, revealed that the Foreign Office knew all about the peace proposals that Sunday morning too.

If the Foreign Office knew, how come Downing Street did not know? If Mr Parkinson knew, how come Mrs Thatcher did not know? Were there, to use the terminology that was later to become familiar during the Westland affair, some 'misunderstandings' between them?

Margaret Thatcher had made up her mind and did not want to be deprived of battle.

I have referred to my meeting with Mrs Thatcher (in the presence of Ian Gow MP) on 21 April 1982. My Parliamentary colleagues know that I said to some of them after the meeting that I had the spine-chilling feeling that she wanted battle, even at that stage. Further evidence of the Prime Minister's state of mind, more eloquent than any assertion of mine, is to be found in the book by Miss Sara Keays. It is no interest of mine, or concern of this narrative, to enter into the relations between Mr Parkinson and Miss Keays. However, this passage from *A Question of Judgement* is very revealing:

> For all the public discussion of settlement proposals, it was clear from what Cecil told me that the Inner Cabinet, like most of the population, privately believed that war was unavoidable.
>
> On Sunday 18 April, Cecil came to see me very late and rather angry. It was the only time I heard him make a serious criticism of the Prime Minister, for whom he had great admiration, being deeply impressed by her courage and determination. He was infuriated by an exchange he had had with her at a meeting of the Inner Cabinet with the Chiefs of Staff. When he had expressed his concern about the risks attendant on a particular course of action, one of several under consideration, she had rounded on him with words to the effect that there was no room for faint-hearts in the Inner Cabinet. I thought it a very telling incident. If the Prime Minister's closest colleagues could not feel free to express their opinions to her absolutely frankly, they could be of no use to her at all.[1]

What the Prime Minister was saying to the House of Commons is crucial to our understanding of her actions,

[1] *A Question of Judgement*, Quintessential Press, 1985.

and her deceit. As late as 1 May, her Foreign Secretary Francis Pym was on what we supposed was a peace mission to Washington. Pym, a holder of the Military Cross, knew what war was, and how unpleasant it could be, and wanted to avoid bloodshed.

On the morning of 2 May he was in close touch with Alexander Haig, who was mediating with the Peruvians. There was a mood of optimism after the news that Galtieri had phoned Belaúnde Terry in the early hours to report his high command's approval, in principle, of the peace proposals' terms. Later, when various minor points had been discussed between Lima, Washington and Buenos Aires, Pym and Haig lunched together.

The implication that the Foreign Secretary was at General Haig's side while all this was going on, and that not a word of it seeped through to Downing Street, is extraordinary. If we are to believe it, it indicates mind-boggling incompetence on the part of the Foreign Office.

By noon agreement looked definite. The last hurdle was a meeting of the Argentine junta at 5 p.m. which would formally approve the proposals. Activity that afternoon in Lima was all geared to the signature of a treaty, bound in red leather, by the British and Argentine Ambassadors that evening. Did Downing Street know nothing about this either? And what were the British Ambassador's instructions? In Lima the President called his press conference to tell the world that a settlement was imminent. Then came the news that the *Belgrano* was sunk.

The final point about the Pym mission is this. When he arrived in Washington on Saturday evening, the Foreign Secretary gave a press conference in which he explained that the British air attacks on the Falklands that day had been intended to concentrate Argentina's mind on a peaceful settlement. On the Sunday morning the War Cabinet meeting at Chequers knew at the very least that Pym was attempting to negotiate. It is against that background that they gave the order to sink an Argentine ship with over 1000 men on board, in circumstances that can only be described as recklessly provocative.

The House of Commons gave its consent for the prosecution of undeclared war on the clear surmise that everything was being done by Her Majesty's Government in good faith to avoid war, and achieve an honourable settlement. In reality, we were grossly deceived. Had the House of Commons known what Sara Keays knew, I doubt whether endorsement would have been forthcoming for the Prime Minister's actions. Certainly any form of bipartisan front-bench approach would have been shattered. Mrs Thatcher won the backing of the House of Commons on a palpably false prospectus.

Let me assume for a moment the role of Devil's Advocate. Reasonable people could say that the Peruvian proposals formed no basis for a long-term solution to the problem of the Falklands. Of them I would ask what other long-term solution to the advantage of Britain is there to be had, other than something based roughly on the Peruvian position, supplemented by that of the United Nations? From the point of view of our country there is *no* long-term military solution, to our advantage, to be had.

What I am about to say may seem a red herring, but there is a nagging question about the wishes of the Falkland Islanders which to date has not been satisfactorily answered. How is it that their perception of Argentina differs so radically from that of the Scots and Welsh communities which have kept their own heritage intact within that country for generations? In 1978 constituents of mine followed the Scottish team to the World Cup. They were, they said, extremely well received by Mr Juan McCafferty and other pillars of the Scots community in Argentina. The Welsh communities in Argentina continue to speak Welsh and play Rugby football without harassment. For all the hard politics of metropolitan Buenos Aires, why should the Falklanders be treated so differently?

Reasonable people could also say that there was no certainty that the Argentines would formally accept the Peruvian proposals. Well, subsequent scholarship reveals not only from Argentine sources, but from American sources, that shortly before the hard-line Admiral Jorge Anaya was hauled out of his junta meeting to be told that his ship had been sunk with loss of life, he was about to put his signature to that acceptance.

But where reasonable people cannot differ is on the crucial issue of the Prime Minister's state of knowledge as to what was going on. When she claims in Parliament that no news of the Peruvian proposals reached London until three hours after the *Belgrano* was sunk,[1] it is simply not true.

We now have to consider the subsequent smokescreen of obfuscation and contradiction that was put up to camouflage the Prime Ministerial sabotage of peace.

On 3 April 1982, in the course of her speech in the fateful Saturday morning Commons debate, I interrupted the Prime Minister to ask who she imagined in South America supported her proposed course of action. The following day I issued a statement from a meeting of West Lothian Constituency Labour Party, saying that the sending of a Task Force to the South Atlantic was the most ill-conceived expedition to leave these shores since the Duke of Buckingham had left for La Rochelle in 1627.[2] Daily thereafter, I made public statements asking for the recall of the Task Force. On Tuesday 4 May (Monday being a public holiday) I asked at the first opportunity whether it was with the Prime Minister's authority that the *Belgrano* had been

[1] Or, more precisely, in her letter to Denzil Davies who had written on behalf of the Shadow Cabinet, that 'the first indications of the Peruvian proposals reached London at 11.15 p.m. on Sunday May 2nd'.

[2] Buckingham sailed to La Rochelle with a British fleet to foment trouble in Aquitaine and Gascony and try to reclaim the heritage of the Plantagenet kings. The expedition was a disaster.

sunk. I did not criticise. War is unpleasant. Unpleasant things happen, whether hostilities are declared or not, and like everyone else in London, I imagined that the Defence Secretary's account of events was truthful. He assured us that the *Belgrano* had been converging on elements of the Task Force, and gave the impression that a submarine commander had had to act, there and then, to protect British ships and lives. This version of events went unchallenged and uncorrected, as long as the hostilities lasted.

It was not until early July that I read in the *Scotsman* newspaper a report by a reliable Scottish journalist, Eric MacKenzie, that he had been sent by his paper to report on the welcome given to HMS *Conqueror* when she returned to Faslane. To a question which was obvious, and flowed from what John Nott had said in the House of Commons – 'Why did you sink the *Belgrano*?' – the submarine commander, Christopher Wreford-Brown, gave an electrifying reply, amplified in the *Aberdeen Press and Journal*. He did not sink the *Belgrano* off his own bat. He was a first-time submarine commander. He did it on orders from Fleet Headquarters at Northwood.

Now this was significantly different from what Parliament, Press, and people had been told. It was only at this point that people began to pay attention to the incident of the *Belgrano*, as opposed to the general issue of the Falklands War. What was the explanation of the discrepancy?

If a clean breast had been made of the matter, and some justification of the contrast between the original statement and the submarine commander's version of his actions had been forthcoming, along the lines that it was necessary to tell lies in time of war in relation to operations, I for one would have accepted such a position. But long after the fighting had ceased, Ministers stuck to untruths when it was obvious that the submarine commander, and not the politicians, was telling the truth. If the real truth had been honourable, why not divulge it after the event?

One point emerged, from Parliamentary questions and

other sources, which was difficult to explain away. That was the course of the *Belgrano*. 280 degrees. West north-west. Heading towards Argentina. Not, as Parliament had been told by John Nott, 'converging on the Task Force'. Again by Parliamentary question I established that there were no elements of the Task Force west of where the *Belgrano* had been sunk. So use of the word 'converging' was downright wrong.

A flurry of different explanations ensued – the precursor of Ministerial and Prime Ministerial behaviour during and after the bombing of Libya. New explanation followed new explanation. When this happens, one can be forgiven for becoming most suspicious.

It was suggested that the course was irrelevant because the old cruiser was zig-zagging. It became clear that she was doing nothing of the kind. She was patrolling up and down outside the Total Exclusion Zone. The Government's confusion about its own imposition of an Exclusion Zone was exposed.

Then I went to a briefing for non-Government MPs at the Ministry of Defence. Admiral Sir Sandy Woodward, the Task Force Commander, looking me hard in the eye, produced a spiel about the Burdwood Bank, and how the *Conqueror* might have lost the *Belgrano* over the Burdwood Bank. How an SSN, a nuclear-powered hunter-killer submarine with highly advanced instrumentation, could possibly lose an old iron-clad is simply mind-boggling. After the briefing, the Library of the House of Commons quickly produced information for me from the maritime experts that the average depth of the Burdwood Bank was 90 fathoms, and the shallowest part 25 fathoms. Now SSNs like the *Conqueror* are built for the eventuality of operating in shallow seas like the Baltic, and it was nonsense for a submariner admiral to try to blind us with guff about his submarine being unable to operate, with its draught of 27 feet, in those waters. In addition, a quick check of the co-ordinates confirmed what I suspected, that the *Belgrano* was nowhere near the Burdwood Bank.

Time and again, this Government has used that old standby trick of blinding its inquisitors with false technical information until they simply give up. But one thing the House of Commons does teach one after a time is to sense when one is being told something that is not quite right.

How was it that I had the confidence to take on Ministers and admirals in areas where it might be assumed that their assertions were paramount? It was because I had been given the diary of Lieutenant Sethia, the supplies officer of the *Conqueror*, recording many crucial details, including the course of the *Belgrano* when she was attacked. Why was I given the diary? Not for the colour of my politics. Not to make trouble for the Royal Navy. But because some people in the Service had come to believe that they had been used. Some of their friends had returned maimed, others had failed to return at all: not for the national interests of our country, but for the political interests of the Prime Minister.

Before I go any further, I wish to answer the charge of wanting to make trouble for the Services. Had that been a motive, I would certainly have exploited the reference in Lt Sethia's diary to the shooting-down of a British helicopter, with the loss of four lives, by HMS *Cardiff*. The mother of the co-pilot, Mrs Cockton, is of the belief that I and others should have demanded the truth about the death of her son as soon as I knew or suspected it. Maybe, in retrospect, Mrs Cockton is correct and justified. I can only say that fifteen months after the event, I did not see what purpose was served by increasing the remorse which must have been felt by the anti-aircraft sailors on a British ship, and the pain felt by the relatives of those who had lost their lives on the helicopter.

Equally, I refused to sign a Commons Early Day Motion asking for an inquiry into the tragedy and possible military error involved in the loss of life among the Welsh Guards as a result of the bombing of *Sir Galahad* at Bluff Cove. Mistakes happen in war, and hindsight is a very wonderful thing. It is no part of the case that I have deployed to criticise retrospectively serving officers and NCOs in the field, in the heat of battle. My complaint is against those in Parliament, sitting on green benches, who sent young men to fight a war which was unnecessary, ill-conceived as to any long-term solution, and devised for bad motives.

There are two other areas of deceit, one comparatively trivial but revealing, the other of cataclysmic importance: the missing Control Room log-book of HMS *Conqueror*, and the taking and conceivable use of nuclear weapons by the Task Force.

News of the loss of the *Conqueror*'s log-book came out of the blue on the BBC morning news the very day that the then Defence Secretary, Michael Heseltine, was due to give evidence to the Select Committee on Foreign Affairs in relation to the *Belgrano*. He was on a sticky wicket due to his insistence on commissioning in March 1984 his own report – the 'Crown Jewels' – on the sinking of the *Belgrano* from his department, where Clive Ponting was the civil servant involved. Timing is of great importance to politicians, and certainly it was a most extraordinary and suspicious coincidence that, in his hour of greatest media need, the Defence Secretary should suddenly discover a dramatic loss which could not reasonably be blamed on him – more reasonably on his predecessor or on the Royal Navy.

What I believe the Control Room log-book might have revealed is the extent to which Ministers and the Prime Minister re-arranged the chronology of events, to dissemble about their own state of knowledge. And it might have indicated the astonishment of the submarine commander that, having followed the *Belgrano* for over thirty hours, he was ordered to sink the iron-clad when she was far less of a potential threat to the Task Force than she had been hours previously. It is my understanding that, so incredulous was he that such an order should be given at that time, he requested confirmation of the orders that had been sent to him. The log-book would have revealed officially that Fleet Headquarters, and surely the Prime Minister, knew that the ship they wished to sink, with the prospect of appalling loss of life before a single British serviceman had been killed in action, was no threat at all.

The search for the log-book has been a cosmetic charade. It culminated in the despatch to the West Indies of Chief Detective Superintendent Ron Hardy and Detective Sergeant Mike Ashdown[1] to interview Lieutenant Mahendra Sethia (whose diary had come into my possession). His assumed media guilt would coincide nicely with the trial at the Old Bailey of Clive Ponting. It would create the general background, favourable to the Government, of an untrustworthy naval diarist in the West Indies and an untrustworthy senior ex-civil servant here at home, about to get their deserts. Hardy and Ashdown, however, were sent by Ministers on what they themselves must have known to be a wild-goose chase. By Parliamentary answer, it is recorded that the Control Room log-book of the *Conqueror* was still on board in October/November 1982. But Sethia had left the Royal Navy in July 1982, and by September was known to be sailing in a yacht with a friend round European waters. Unless he had returned surreptitiously to his old submarine, in order to purloin the log-book in the dead of night, he could not have been guilty. Sending the detectives (and in no way were the policemen themselves to blame) was a gross abuse of taxpayers' money.

In the public mind, the mystery of the missing log-book remains. In my mind, there is no mystery. The Control Room log-book of HMS *Conqueror* never went missing. As one crew member of the *Conqueror*, now retired from the Navy, put it to me, with suitable expletives which I have deleted: 'If you think that any of us would have pinched the ******* log-book from the ******* control room of the only ******* nuclear submarine ever to have

[1] At a cost to the taxpayer of £6,940.80.

been used in action by any ******* country, to put on our ******* sideboard for a ******* memento – you must be ******* daft!' As he rightly pointed out, it would have been a court-martial offence, and the debriefing on the *Conqueror*'s return was most efficient and careful, to the highest standards expected of the Royal Navy.

I concede that it is probably true that the *Conqueror*'s log did not end up at Fleet Headquarters, Northwood. I concede it did not end up as it should have done in the Records Department of Naval Establishment at Hayes, Middlesex. I assert that it is so politically sensitive, not because of what it contains but on account of the political usefulness of its 'disappearance', that it was sent to the Ministry of Defence itself, almost unique among records, and there it remains.

Hideously and spine-chillingly worse was the deceit over nuclear weapons.

Britain (though not Argentina) had signed Protocol One of the Treaty of Tlatelolco under which nuclear weapons were not to be used in the South Atlantic. Moreover, the British Foreign Office had boasted that it led the way in proclaiming that our country would never threaten to use, let alone use nuclear weapons against a non-nuclear power. In the event our non-nuclear posturing proved to be empty.

From the Mediterranean, nuclear depth charges certainly went south. Michael Flockhart of Leith, the shop steward on board the Royal Fleet Auxiliary *Fort Austin*, has told the National Union of Seamen that on 28 March 1982 members of the crew of the *Fort Austin* went ashore at Gibraltar. They were informed by the local barmaids that instead of going north and home to Britain after five months in the sweltering Gulf, they were going straight to the South Atlantic. (One question arises as to how the barmaids of Gibraltar had better information about the destination of the Fleet with nuclear weapons than the British Prime Minister!)

The young officer from HMS *Glamorgan*, author posthumously of the moving diaries *A Message from the Falklands*, edited by his father Professor Hugh Tinker,[1] records that he was amazed to go on board the Royal Fleet Auxiliary and find dummy nuclear weapons. But of course there were dummy nuclear weapons, since there would have to have been dummies for practice in moving the weapons between ship and helicopter. Besides, Keith Speed, Member of Parliament for Ashford and Navy Minister sacked by Mrs Thatcher, has said that he would have been astonished had not the Fleet from the Mediterranean been carrying nuclear weapons.

From Portsmouth and Devonport nuclear weapons were taken, although Professor Sir Ronald Mason, Chief Scientist at the Ministry of Defence, and others have said that they tried hard and partially succeeded in bringing back some of the nuclear weapons before the Fleet left the Western Approaches.

That brave man Petty Officer Michael Harrison was given his Queen's Gallantry Medal not as the press suggested – the citation was more careful – for going into the tomb of HMS *Coventry* to rescue code books which would have been destroyed by sea water, but to determine what could be done about emissions of radio-nucleides from weaponry sunk with the cruiser.

Far more serious, however, are the issues arising from the fact that an 'R' Class submarine – that is, a Polaris submarine – went 21 degrees West, 12 degrees South, out of range of the Soviet Union, and within range of Argentina. I am told by Professor John Erickson, Professor of Defence Studies at the University of Edinburgh, and others, that it would be frivolous to send one fifth of our so-called nuclear deterrent simply for the use of her torpedo tubes. Such a decision could only have been taken as an *in extremis* option, with a view to conceivable use. Not only in the House of Commons

[1] *A Message From the Falklands: The Life and Gallant Death of David Tinker, Lieut., RN*, Penguin Books, 1983.

were there many Conservative MPs who were talking openly about the possibility of having to use our nuclear capability, but I believe there were those in the Navy who contemplated such action might be necessary. Politicians and proud naval officers, facing possible humiliation and defeat, could resort to mad and immoral decisions. What we are talking about is Hiroshima-plus in the South Atlantic, in the course of a war described by General Haig as 'like two bald men fighting over a comb'. Certainly in the period between the loss of the *Sheffield* and the landing at San Carlos, I know that the Prime Minister was warned by senior naval officers that the loss of one major unit – the *Canberra*, the *Hermes* or the *Invincible* – would render the task of re-possessing the Falkland Islands impossible. I am told that she replied to the Navy that defeat was unthinkable and that we might have to teach the Argentines a lesson – with the implication that the lesson could be a nuclear response. If this is thought fanciful, one only has to turn again to the Tinker diaries where the young lieutenant, shortly to be killed on board *Glamorgan*, writes, '———— even said, "Drop a big white job (Polaris) on them." Thank God he's not in command.'[1]

As on the *Belgrano*, and as on so much else, the Government have refused to answer questions, taking sanctuary in the 'need for secrecy' and allowing the storm of public opinion to abate as newspapers and television have inevitably gone on to consider other matters.

Timing is everything in politics. And though the tactic of allowing the storm to abate has generally served the Prime Minister well, there have been two moments when Mrs Thatcher's deception was so far uncovered that she could have been knocked out of Number Ten Downing Street.

[1] *A Message from the Falklands*: p. 168.

One, as we shall see, was during the Commons debate on the Law Officer's letter during the Westland affair, when the wrong speech for the occasion by Neil Kinnock let the Prime Minister off the proverbial hook. The other was in the aftermath of the famous television interview with Mrs Diana Gould, housewife of Cirencester, and Cambridge geography graduate, on the *Nationwide* programme hosted by Sue Lawley on 24 May 1983.

Mrs Gould began by asking: 'Mrs Thatcher, why, when the *Belgrano*, the Argentinian battleship, was outside of the exclusion zone and actually sailing away from the Falklands, why did you give the orders to sink it?'

Mrs Thatcher replied that the *Belgrano* was not sailing away from the Falklands. 'It was in an area which was a danger to our ships, and to our people on them.'

All the arguments followed: the changing of the rules of engagement, the questions of danger and threat, the actual course and position of the cruiser. Mrs Gould knew her facts, and stubbornly stuck to them.

Mrs Thatcher's appeal, however, ignored facts in favour of patriotic duty. 'When it was sunk, that ship was a danger to our ships. My duty was to look after our troops, our ships, our Navy. And, my goodness me, I lived with many, many anxious days and nights.'

Mrs Gould was not satisfied, rightly. She asked Mrs Thatcher to correct her first answer in which she had said that the cruiser was *not* sailing away from the Falklands. The Prime Minister could not. She could only evade the truth by reiterating the danger to the Navy, and offering the full facts 'in about thirty years' time'.

Sue Lawley asked Mrs Gould: 'What motive are you seeking to attach to Mrs Thatcher and her Government? Is it inefficiency, lack of communication? Or is it a desire for action, a desire for war?'

'It is a desire for action, and a lack of communication,' said Mrs Gould. Without prompting, she had found the answer. 'Because giving those orders to sink the *Belgrano* when it was sailing *away* from our fleet, and *away* from the Falklands, was in effect sabotaging any possibility of any peace plan succeeding.'

Afterwards, Mrs Gould discovered from *Nationwide* that the Prime Minister had been very upset and said that 'such questioning of a Prime Minister could only happen in a democracy'. Mrs Gould did 'not know why she felt she had to say this'.[1] It is indeed a highly puzzling utterance.

As the best biography that I have read of Margaret Thatcher, by Bruce Arnold, put it, 'Truth wrestled with fact, in that *Nationwide* exchange on May 24, and truth triumphed. Margaret Thatcher told a lie. Just one. But a lie, nonetheless, visible, inescapable, related to an issue that should have been part of the [election] campaign, but had been hardly mentioned.'[2]

All those who saw the programme are agreed that it was the one moment during the General Election of 1983 when the Prime Minister looked uncomfortable. Yet it was not followed up. The explanation is simple. Most of us who might have followed it up did *not* see the programme, as we were out canvassing or at meetings in the summer evening. Equally, the Labour Party in my view was nervous about the whole issue of the Falklands and did not wish to harp on the subject – though the mind boggles at what the press would have done to a Labour Prime Minister who was exposed as Mrs Thatcher was by Mrs Gould.

This is a strange tale that I am about to tell. I have never been able to resist the feeling that it is, at the last, a ghost story.

In early December 1983, I was told by a source whose identity I made a most solemn promise not to reveal, that 'Mrs Thatcher knew bloody well that those ships were going home'. Those ships were the *Belgrano*, and her

[1] *On the Spot: The Sinking of the Belgrano* by Diana Gould, Cecil Woolf, 1984.
[2] *Margaret Thatcher: A Study in Power*, Hamish Hamilton, 1984.

escorts the *Piedra Buena* and the *Hipolito Bouchard*.

Precisely how did she know? I asked.

'Well, how do you think?' the source replied. 'Through GCHQ, of course.'

At that point, I must confess, I had the haziest notion only that there was a major communications centre in the Cheltenham area. Even for Defence-oriented MPs, GCHQ was an elusive subject of which we knew little. Naturally I then asked: What exactly did the Prime Minister know? My source demurred. To give me too much information might lead to exposure, and the wrecking of career.

But the source was also deeply angry, and had reason to trust me. So the source compromised. 'What Mrs Thatcher knew at Chequers that morning [Sunday 2 May] was that an order had gone out from the operational commander – Admiral Allara – on board the carrier *Veinticinco de Mayo*, ordering the *Belgrano* and escorts back to Staten Island on the coast of Argentina. And that this order was confirmed by the Naval Command in Buenos Aires at 1.19 a.m. on that Sunday. The bitch knew that the *Belgrano* was no threat to her Task Force,' I was told in cool, calculated anger.[1]

The ramifications of this information hit me between the eyes. Assuming what I was told was true and accurate, the villainy of the Prime Minister was deep. Remember that no British serviceman had lost his life in action before the *Belgrano* was sunk.

But I am always reluctant to rely on a single source, however trustworthy I judge it to be. So I made enquiries of friends of mine who had sailed with the Task Force. It was clear that the AD470 high-frequency Marconi transceiver equipment on board ships of the Task Force had intercepted most Argentine messages, and flashed them back to Ascension Island, whence they were relayed to Cheltenham and decrypted.

[1] I will add only two facts about the source. The source was in a position to know, and was *not* Clive Ponting.

By the winter of 1983, I had established many contacts over the Falklands, and two of them told me that they were 'almost certain' that the same information about the orders at 8.07 p.m. and 1.19 a.m. had come through Chile. Other contacts expressed themselves as absolutely certain that Mrs Thatcher had the content of the orders to the *Belgrano* through the Americans, via their satellite in polar orbit.

So I went to the Commons Table Office with questions on GCHQ.

At this point, I should explain that there is a duty roster of four Clerks of the House, usually in their mid-thirties, two of whom sit in the Table Office from 10 a.m. to the rising of the House. Service in the Table Office will usually cover three or four years of a Clerk's career, and it is virtually an obligatory step for any Clerk who wishes to be promoted to the higher echelons. The Clerks in the Table Office are, without exception in my experience, extremely clever and helpful people, whose duty it is to help MPs frame their questions, provided that the Member knows in his own mind what he wants to know. The rules for questions involve Ministerial responsibility, and contrary to general public belief these rules are very tight.

Late one night in mid-December 1983, I went into the Table Office with the question, 'To ask the Prime Minister at what time, on Sunday 2 May 1982, she received information from GCHQ about intercepted orders to the *Belgrano* on Saturday evening/Sunday morning 1/2 May; and if she will make a statement.' The duty Clerk, Robert Rodgers, currently Clerk of the Defence Committee and a philologist by background, ruled the question out of order on several grounds. MPs cannot ask about Intelligence matters. MPs cannot ask about matters which the Table Office judge to be 'history' – and history often starts last year for such purposes. I thought I was stymied. So, Robert, I said, what on earth can I ask? Reflecting, he vouchsafed that there were only two matters which would be 'orderly' – the green light for getting Parliamentary

Questions on the Order Paper. 'You can ask the Prime Minister about Ministerial responsibility, and you could ask her, I suppose, about the polygraphs.'

This was an afterthought by the Clerk that I believe has reverberating effects to this day. In the autumn of 1983 there had been some controversy about the use of lie detectors, the so-called polygraph. Robert Rodgers seemed to know, though I didn't, that the polygraph question had surfaced at Cheltenham. At that point I had no notion that the trade unions at Cheltenham were complaining about the imposition of polygraphs.

Such was the genesis of two Written Answers, buried in Hansard of 19 December 1983:

Government Communications Headquarters

Mr Dalyell asked the Prime Minister at what cost she is introducing six polygraphs at Government Communications Headquarters, Cheltenham.

The Prime Minister: The Security Commission recommended a pilot scheme covering the security service at the Government Communications Headquarters to test the feasibility of polygraph examinations in the context of security screening. Equipment for this purpose has been purchased at a cost of US $25,000.

Mr Dalyell asked the Prime Minister if responsibility for Government Communications Headquarters, Cheltenham remains with the Secretary of State for Foreign and Commonwealth Affairs.

The Prime Minister: Yes.

Remember – these questions appeared at a time when 600 Members of the House of Commons would have been quite blank, if asked what or where GCHQ was.

The scene shifts from the Table Office of the House of Commons to a draughty school hall on a snowy winter's night, 12 January 1984, in Saltcoats on the Ayrshire coast. I had been invited by the Cunninghame North and Cunninghame South Constituency Labour Parties to speak at a public meeting. Astonishingly, given the weather, there were about 150 people present. Hugh MacMahon, later Strathclyde West MEP and local deputy headmaster, was in the chair, and my friend and Parliamentary colleague, David Lambie MP, was on the platform beside me. His wife, Mrs Netta Lambie, Provost of Saltcoats, Councillor Willie Goudie, and many other people well-known in the life of North Ayrshire were present.

After I had spoken, as always I took questions. The third question of the evening did not come in the rich accents of the West of Scotland. It was very precise.

'Mr Dalyell, how exactly do you know that the Prime Minister knew about the orders to the *Belgrano* to return to Argentine territorial waters?'

I cannot pretend to remember the exact wording of my reply, but it was to the effect that it was 'through GCHQ at Cheltenham' and via transmission from the Task Force to Ascension Island, probably also through Chile, and certainly from Washington.

After the meeting, I asked my hosts who it was who had asked that particular question. All remembered the question and answer very clearly – and still do. But not one of the members of the Saltcoats–Ardrossan or other Labour Parties knew or had ever seen the man who put the question. The local press were equally puzzled. North Ayrshire is a community in which local personages know everyone (and most likely know their business, too). It was unlikely to the point of being almost inconceivable that a man would come to such a Labour Party public meeting, and ask a question like that without a purpose. I wondered aloud at the time whether he was from the Intelligence services.

That was 12 January. On Wednesday 25 January, I was unusually not in the House of Commons for Questions, since I had been the guest of the Bristol University Labour

Club at a lunchtime students' meeting. In the afternoon, before going on to an evening meeting of the Salisbury Labour Party, I was shown round the Wills Physics Laboratory in Bristol. Emerging from the Laboratory, I was asked for my comments by a reporter on the announcement of the banning of trade unions at the Communications Centre at Cheltenham. The what? I said.

This came out of the blue. I said in Salisbury that evening that, had I been in the House, I would have asked there and then about the possible connection with the *Belgrano* messages, and what had happened in Saltcoats thirteen days earlier.

Geoffrey Howe had made a short statement after Foreign Office Questions. 'I have today signed certificates under section 121(4) of the Employment Protection Act 1975 and section 138(4) of the Employment Protection (Consolidation) Act 1978, excepting GCHQ employees from the application of the relevant provision. Under those new conditions, staff will be permitted in future to belong only to a departmental staff association approved by their director.' I am told by my friends and colleagues present that they could never recollect such a sense of bewilderment in the House. This was not confined to the Opposition. Even the Secretary of State for Employment, Tom King, let it be known that he had not been consulted.

One MP who did know something about GCHQ was Denis Healey, for six years Defence Secretary. He found Sir Geoffrey's statement disturbing and perplexing. Referring to the Geoffrey Prime case of 1982, as far as he was aware there had been no action against anyone employed at GCHQ for three years. What consultations were there? Had the measure been referred to the Security Commission who were set up precisely to consider such issues?

Howe replied that Members of the Security Commission were not consulted. 'It is not a matter for them. They are normally involved only in cases where there has been a breach of security.' No, the trade unions were not consulted. Howe then referred back to the industrial action which had taken place in 1979–81.

But the question, which has never been answered, is that if the Government were worried about what happened up to 1981, is it not a dereliction of duty on their part not to have acted earlier, if they thought this drastic action were justified?

Why not have a no-strike agreement? asked Dr David Owen, reasonably enough. Such an agreement could not prevent exposure to industrial tribunals, opined Howe lamely. Experience had also shown, he added, that in an organisation whose activities include Intelligence work there can be problems if staff are members of national trade unions. This created real anger, at the implied slur that trade unionists were unpatriotic.

Local and independent Conservative MP Charles Irving was furious with his Government. 'Staff at GCHQ are already reeling,' he said, 'under the imposition for a trial period of the lie detector, which is renowned for its failure rate.' Seven thousand people in his constituency were involved. 'I can assure my Hon. Friend,' said the Foreign Secretary, 'that the matter I have announced today has no connection with the Government's acceptance of the Security Commission's recommendation that a pilot scheme should be carried out to test the feasibility of polygraph examinations.'

Well, if it was not to do with the polygraph, what was it about? If there was no security leak worth reporting to the Security Commission, queried Dr John Gilbert, former Defence Minister, why was it necessary? Platitudes were all he got in return. Former Home Secretary, Merlyn Rees, declared: 'Governments do not usually act in this way unless something has happened. Has anything happened recently, or has any information been received?' More generalities about having thought long and hard from the Foreign Secretary. Dr Gavin Strang asked: 'Does it not suggest that the decision reflects the Government's hostility to British trade unionism rather than to any need to protect our national interests?' Nothing of the kind, contended the Foreign Secretary, Dr Strang could not be more wrong. How many shop stewards, asked Dennis Skinner, had betrayed their country, compared to Eton and Harrow? 'Freedom is threatened by Fascism,' was Sir Geoffrey's non-answer. Justifiably could Denis Healey observe that the Foreign Secretary's attempt to justify his action had increased rather than allayed concern. A shabby affair. An imprudent action.

Four years later, the GCHQ cause rumbles on. No convincing explanation has been offered to this day why, at that moment, long after the Geoffrey Prime case, which might possibly have furnished some excuse, the Foreign Secretary and the Prime Minister decided on this course of action. They hardly sat down on a January afternoon, and said to one another over a cup of tea, 'What shall we do tomorrow – bash the unions at Cheltenham?'

Something sparked it off. Until it is shown to the contrary, I shall believe it was that question on 19 December 1983 to the Prime Minister on the polygraph. Anxious that her iniquitous behaviour on the *Belgrano* be exposed, I am told that Mrs Thatcher was as 'obsessed with the *Belgrano*' as I was. When she got the question about GCHQ, the first ever, I believe, and saw that it related to polygraphs, she and her closest advisers put two and two together – reasonably enough, but in fact wrongly. 'It's those trade unionists with their polygraph complaints that have been talking to that awful Tam Dalyell about the signals which came to me on 1/2 May 1982.' I suspect that the whole GCHQ announcement – without, I reiterate, even consultation with Cabinet colleagues entitled to know, was a crude attempt to put the frighteners on suspected sources and stop them producing the proof that she had lied about the *Belgrano*.

There is a host of reasons for returning to the Falklands, such as the continuing costs,[1] and the possibility of a replay from macho men who have been humiliated: the election of a civilian President does not mean the Argentine military have simply gone away. But one reason above all concerns this book. If Members of Parliament simply shrug our shoulders and say let bygones be bygones, this Prime Minister will try it again. I am not a great one for standing on the dignity of MPs, or the rights of the House of Commons, but if the elected representatives of the people allow themselves to be lied to, and do nothing about it, then do we not injure democracy itself? Once the Government got away with the *Belgrano*, a number of episodes have occurred which it has managed to contain. No other British Government has ever been so successful.

[1] The cost of the Falklands campaign and subsequent expenditure in 1982–83 was £780 million. The cost of garrisoning the islands has been running at between £250 million and £400 million a year for the past four years. The cost of replacing ships and equipment lost is still approximately £200 million a year. Total costs from 1982–87 are over £3 billion, or more than £1.5 million for every man, woman and child on the islands.

2

Lying With a Letter

This is not a matter of honest differences of policy choices between Cabinet Ministers over the future of the Westland helicopter company. Such differences have certainly existed in all Cabinets on many issues.

This is about deceit.

The Government was proclaiming one policy in public – their neutrality about the future ownership of the company – while another policy was being pursued in private, that is, backing a takeover by the American Sikorsky firm.

Yet again, this Government was deceiving Parliament, press, and people about their real policy. Throughout. the Westland story, the central question of deceit and partisanship arose on several occasions and in a number of extraordinary contexts.

Ever since the summer of 1985, anxieties had been growing both at the Westland plants and in their boardroom about the lack of orders for the future. In December 1985 the crisis came to a head when Westland found itself the target of two takeover bids, one from the American Sikorsky firm, the other from a European consortium.

Mrs Thatcher favoured the Americans. Mr Heseltine suddenly developed warm enthusiasm for the European option. Much was to happen before a row was precipitated in Cabinet, but the central event was a letter from the Solicitor General to Mr Heseltine alleging inaccuracies in a letter he had written to David Horne, the managing director of Lloyds Merchant Bank who were representing the consortium's interest.[1]

Complexity has been one of the Prime Minister's most effective allies, in concealing her wrongdoing from the British people. Attempting to unravel and make sense of the Westland affair is best done by examining the events through the roles of the *dramatis personae*.

The young pretender

Michael Heseltine, shamelessly and honourably ambitious, President of the Oxford Union, publisher and politician, darling of the Conservative Party Conference, had long been perceived as a contender for the top job in Number Ten Downing Street. Almost inevitably, therefore, one could not expect a close relationship between Mrs Thatcher and her flamboyant Defence Secretary. On the other hand, he had served her well in the Department of the Environment, and had stepped into John Nott's shoes as Defence Secretary at an awkward time for the Government. Mrs Thatcher had given him full backing on a number of delicate issues, such as the handling of CND and the Propaganda Unit in the Ministry of Defence, DS 19,[2] and the investigation into the apparent leak of top secret information in 1984 from the GCHQ signals base at Ayios Nikolaos in Cyprus, by personnel of 9 Signals Regiment.

However, in the spring of 1984 Michael Heseltine knew he had to go before the Select Committee on Foreign Affairs over the events of 1 and 2 May 1982, and serious disagreements emerged between him and Margaret Thatcher as to how the decision to sink the *Belgrano* should be handled. He eventually appeared before the Select Committee on 7 November 1984, but not before questions

---

[1] The Solicitor General's letter is quoted in full in the Appendix.
[2] Set up specifically by the Defence Secretary to deal with CND.

were raised in Downing Street about his loyalty to his leader.

My questions, thick and fast, on the *Belgrano* had prompted him to commission a full report on the sinking from the Ministry of Defence civil servant Clive Ponting, colloquially known as the 'Crown Jewels'. But Michael Heseltine was rather too blunt for his own good about his reasons for doing so. If he was to protect the Government's position, said he, he needed to know exactly what had happened throughout the *Belgrano* sinking, and he informed Number Ten exactly what he was doing – not least because the civil service network would have told the Cabinet Secretary, Sir Robert Armstrong, anyway.

However, the particular phrase that he used was tactless in the extreme, and sent the Prime Minister through the roof with rage when she heard it from other senior Conservatives to whom Michael Heseltine had freely used it: 'I want to be quite sure that there is not a Watergate in this somewhere.' In the corridors of the House of Commons, the gossips were not slow to realise that if Michael Heseltine thought there might be a Watergate around, it must mean the thought had occurred to the Defence Secretary that there was a potential Richard Nixon around in the form of the lady in Number Ten Downing Street. From this point on, the *modus vivendi* between Mrs Thatcher and Michael Heseltine was strained.

On 18 November 1985, I was due to speak at an evening meeting of the Bridport Labour Party in Dorset. So, having heard constantly over a period of a few months, during meetings of the ASTMS Group of Labour MPs, about the union's anxieties over Westland Helicopters, I arranged to go to Yeovil in the afternoon.

The management extended every courtesy to me, and I was taken round by Captain Bill Gueterbock, the public relations director, and by Mr Bill Howell, one of the senior shop stewards. Both management and unions emphasised the plight of the company and its desperate desire to win orders. But they did more than that. They pleaded with me to try to get Ministers, particularly at the Department of Defence, to take some interest in the increasingly critical situation at Yeovil. They wrung their proverbial hands at the absence of Ministerial concern about the future of the British helicopter industry.

So the inevitable question arises – what on earth happened between the third week of November and the first week of December 1985 to transform Ministerial indifference into a resigning issue for a senior Cabinet Minister?

The real answer must seem at first hand to be irrational. Early in December 1985, another issue had surfaced in acute form, in the highest echelons of the British Government. This was British participation in the American Strategic Defence Initiative programme, popularly but misleadingly dubbed 'Star Wars'. Certainly the substantive decision about, and possibly even the Prime Minister's first public announcement of, British participation in SDI was made without proper consultation with the responsible Cabinet Minister, the Defence Secretary Michael Heseltine. On or about 5 December 1985, Michael Heseltine was peremptorily summoned to Number Ten, and told by Mrs Thatcher in no uncertain terms to bury his doubts about SDI, and the doubts of some of his chief advisers in the Ministry of Defence. British participation in SDI was her agreement with President Reagan, and he could like it or lump it.

Smarting with anger at the way in which he had been treated by his Prime Minister, Michael Heseltine lumped it on that occasion and issue.

The subsequent strictures which Michael Heseltine was to pile on the style in which Mrs Thatcher ran her Cabinet originated from her treatment of him over this vastly important strategic issue for East and West, rather than over the fate of a relatively small helicopter firm in the West Country.

But, as so often in public life, rows flare up over purported issues somewhat removed from the real issues which are the true source of the trouble. This scenario goes some way to explain Michael Heseltine's subsequent behaviour. It also perhaps goes some way to explain Prime Ministerial petulance, and the irritation of Mrs Thatcher as to why the Cabinet was spending so much time on a small firm, valued at £30 million, when there were so many other things to discuss – until January 1986, when she realised with dismay that the small matter of Westland plc threatened to engulf her entire Government.

In early January 1986, it looked as if Mr Heseltine's real complaint was not so much about helicopters, let alone SDI, as about Mrs Thatcher's determination to get her way, and in so doing busting that sacred, if ill-defined, thing, the British constitution. The full enormity of Mr Heseltine's charge against the Prime Minister became clear in his article in the *Observer* of 12 January. Implicitly answering the widely expressed criticism that the Westland affair was pretty small beer to have precipitated such a hugely damaging political row, Michael Heseltine wrote: 'What was much more important to me was the emergence of what I consider to be the breakdown of constitutional government. That was something I could not live with. There was, therefore, no option for me but to resign.'

Now that really is a pretty spectacular charge for a Minister to make against his Prime Minister. Mr Heseltine expanded on it under robust questioning from Brian Walden on the *Weekend World* television programme at lunchtime that Sunday. The burden of his case was that Mrs Thatcher had failed to win support for her view of the Westland affair from a majority of what he called 'the colleagues' who attended two Cabinet Committee meetings on the subject early in December. She again failed to get support at a third meeting on the subject, and ended up with a declaration that they would meet again four days later. Then, according to Mr Heseltine, the Prime Minister realised that she would do no better at a fourth meeting and unilaterally cancelled it. It was this cancellation which Mr Heseltine claims amounted to a breach of our unwritten constitution. For in effect it deprived the 'colleagues' – the rest of the Cabinet – of the opportunity to consider, and make up their minds between his view of the Westland affair and the Prime Minister's. In Mr Heseltine's view, she was imposing her will in defiance of the majority of her Cabinet.

There has been subsequent argument as to whether this fourth meeting was in fact ever promised by Mrs Thatcher. Downing Street claimed that there was nothing definite about what the Prime Minister said. Mr Heseltine stuck to his version, pointing out that civil servants who had heard the Prime Minister's pledge had acted upon it by beginning the arrangements for such a meeting. These civil servants had only hauled off when Mrs Thatcher told them that the meeting was off. I find Mr Heseltine's version the more believable of the two, and I have had it confirmed to my satisfaction from sources with a good track record of accuracy.

Whether the mystery of the disappearing meeting amounts to a monstrous breach of the rules of Cabinet Government and a breakdown of the constitution is doubtful. I am inclined to the view that it is, instead, another example of the dirty tactics Mrs Thatcher uses when she is determined to get her way: a blatantly off-the-ball foul, but not vastly different from her normal behaviour as a conviction – that is, pig-headed – politician.

The faithful courtier

If Michael Heseltine gave up office too impetuously, the same cannot be said of Leon Brittan. He clung on for as long as possible, and even after his enforced departure continued to give the supreme service of any politician to his Prime Minister – that of silence.

Perhaps the final straw for Leon Brittan was the memorable phrase which was uttered at the crucial moment by Roy Jenkins, proving that the *mot juste* can still seal the fate of a politician. As Leon Brittan teetered on the brink of resignation, Jenkins effectively ejected him from office by arguing that while his explanation of events came just within the bounds of the truth, 'the margin is so narrow that we will count our spoons very quickly whenever they are together'. That had its effect on the cumulative anxieties of his Parliamentary colleagues, and it was their withdrawal of confidence rather than any wrongdoing which Leon Brittan gave as a reason for his departure from the Cabinet. He never said – nor probably felt – he had done anything wrong. He was going because 'I no longer command the full confidence of my colleagues'.

It was pressure from Conservative backbenchers which forced Leon Brittan to follow Michael Heseltine out of the Government, not the requirements of Ministerial responsibility. And it was the need to preserve the position of the Prime Minister, and not constitutional doctrine, that led the Conservative majority on the House of Commons Select Committee on Defence to 'clear' Mrs Thatcher and vent their spleen on Mr Brittan instead.

I ought to state frankly that, as the MP who contributed crucially to Leon Brittan's current (though I believe temporary) downfall by naming Colette Bowe, I have sympathy with the predicament in which he found himself. Of all people in the Government, Leon Brittan, Double First at Cambridge in English and Law, a successful QC, a former Home Secretary, was sensitive to the enormous importance of a Law Officer's letters. Of all Ministers, he would be and was sensitive to the reckless hazards of leaking such a letter. He acquiesced in the leak only to please the Prime Minister, against all his own instincts. (It is relevant that Leon Brittan had been promoted to the position of youngest Home Secretary in memory by Mrs Thatcher, without much following or power base in the Tory Party, and relied on her patronage.)

The detailed mechanics of the circumstances in which Leon Brittan agreed to the leaking of the Mayhew letter by his Department of Trade and Industry, need not detain us. What *is* important was that in his mind he was acting at the behest of the Prime Minister and her press secretary, Mr Bernard Ingham. And the proof is to be found in the resignation correspondence.

In a quarter of a century as a Member of Parliament, I have seen many resignation letters between Prime Ministers and those departing from the Government. Some have been affectionate, as between old friends and political colleagues who have been together in party or movement for years. Others have been sad. Others curt. Some acrimonious. Never, ever has there been a correspondence like that between Margaret Thatcher and her departing Trade Secretary:

24 January 1986

My Dear Prime Minister,

Since your statement in the House yesterday it has become clear to me that I no longer command the full confidence of my colleagues.

In these circumstances, my continued membership of your Government would be a source of weakness rather than strength and, as I have explained to you, it is for this reason that I have tendered my resignation.

It has been an honour and a privilege to serve in your Government successfully as Minister of State at the Home Office, as Chief Secretary to the Treasury, as Home Secretary and as Secretary of State for Trade and Industry.

I shall, of course, continue to give the Government my full support from the backbenches.

It is above all vital that the crucial work of national regeneration which we were all elected to achieve should continue unimpeded.

Yours
Leon

My Dear Leon,

I am very sorry that despite all the arguments I could use I was unable to dissuade you this afternoon from resigning. As I told you, I have received in recent hours many messages of support for you from Parliamentary colleagues. It was my wish that you should remain as a member of the Cabinet. But I have respect for your decision.

I have greatly valued you as a Cabinet colleague, as Chief Secretary of the Treasury, Home Secretary and as Secretary of State for Trade and Industry. We shall all miss you. You have been a steadfast exponent of Government policy and I have admired the dedication and loyalty with which you have carried out your duties. I hope that it will not be long before you return to high office to continue your Ministerial career.

Yours ever,
Margaret

How with sincerity, and propriety, could she have had the wish that Leon Brittan should remain a member of the Cabinet if he alone had been responsible for all these dreadful happenings? How could she have expressed the hope that it would not be long before he returned to high office to continue his Ministerial career, if the whole story had been of a Secretary of State who had deceived his senior civil servants, his Cabinet Secretary, and his Prime Minister for fourteen long days? It is inconceivable that the Prime Minister would have been allowed by Number Ten, or wished herself, to write in such terms.

The truth is that Leon Brittan negotiated the correspondence. Without some kind of public assurance, he would have spilled the beans and not been persuaded to act as the sacrificial scapegoat. Had not such a letter been forthcoming, Leon Brittan might have refused to carry the can for the Prime Minister. He was in a position to negotiate. As Simon Jenkins had it in the *Sunday Times*, from an informed source, 'Passages had to be negotiated with Leon Brittan, lest he step out of line in the debate.'

For my part, I do not think the British House of Commons should be content at all with being given a 'line'. The House of Commons is entitled to the truth, and if we allow ourselves to accept a line unquestioningly, then we are simply not doing our job properly.

One of the most amazing mornings and afternoons of twenty-five years in the House was on 29 January 1986, when I sat in the Committee Room listening to Leon Brittan steadfastly refusing to answer questions from the Select Committee on Defence about the planning of the leak and the extent of the Prime Minister's knowledge. When he was pressed by the chairman, Sir Humphrey Atkins, by my colleagues Dick Douglas and John Gilbert, and by his own colleagues, he was forced into the humiliating position of an American wrongdoer having to plead the Fifth Amendment. Question upon question cascaded down on him, and he refused point-blank to answer. When did he first discuss the need to leak the letter with Number Ten Downing Street? Who authorised the selective passages for leaking? Why, according to the Prime Minister, had he said not a word about his role to her, until the enquiry let out the truth that *he* had authorised the leak?

The only explanation is that the responsibility was higher up – since Brittan, to his credit, was not prepared to see any of his departmental officials taking the blame. As Dr David Owen commented at the time, 'The affair is a spider's web, and as each strand of the web is unravelled, we get closer to the spider's nest, which is Number Ten and the spider herself is the Prime Minister.'

I am confirmed in this view by an account I have been given of the Friday morning meeting at 8.30 a.m. in the Department of Trade and Industry on the day of Leon Brittan's resignation. He chaired the meeting of his advisers, attended by Ministers in his Department, Gerry Malone, his Parliamentary Private Secretary, and DTI civil servants. What to do about his future? He canvassed opinion, as he might have done at any of a hundred departmental conferences. Views pro and con resignation were asked for in a very cool and impressive way that won the admiration of some of those present. After all, here was a young Cabinet Minister discussing his own demise.

I am told it was the MPs present who thought that Brittan could not hold out, weather the storm and regain authority, and would therefore have to go. They had been getting all the House of Commons gossip the night before. And from the morning papers they discerned that Bernard Ingham had been weighing in against Brittan remaining, which was indeed Vatican's black smoke. By contrast, the officials, to a man, were in favour of his remaining, and none more clearly so than Sir Brian Hayes, the permanent secretary. So what is the explanation?

It can only be deduced that the permanent secretary and senior officials knew full well that responsibility for the leak lay elsewhere than with their Department and their Secretary of State. I do not believe for one moment that out of politeness, sycophancy, or personal regard, Sir Brian Hayes would have urged Leon Brittan to remain, if he thought that he, his colleagues, other Cabinet Ministers, and the Prime Minister had been deceived by Leon Brittan. Hayes would have said, 'You must go.' It speaks volumes that he took no such attitude.

Our learned friends

Under the by-line of the careful, well-informed, then political correspondent of the *Sunday Telegraph*, Mr John Lewis, there appeared on the front page of the *Sunday Telegraph* of 27 July 1986, the headline, 'Havers threat to call police to Number 10'. Sir Michael Havers was compelled, claimed Lewis, 'to warn Sir Robert Armstrong, the Cabinet Secretary, at the height of the Westland Affair that he would have the police on the doorstep of Number 10 next morning, unless he agreed to an immediate leaks inquiry'. Here was the senior Law Officer of the Crown, returning from his sick-bed, and threatening to send the Constabulary to the doorstep of Number Ten, hardly an everyday occurrence.

The correspondence which I print below, between the Attorney General and the Shadow Attorney General, the Right Hon. John Morris QC MP, Member of Parliament for Aberavon, is a classic example of non-answer to legitimate questions:

To the Rt Hon. Sir Michael Havers QC MP:

31 October 1986

Dear Michael

I have been asked by the Parliamentary Committee to write to you concerning the answer you gave to Tam Dalyell on 14 July 1986 (Hansard Column 675) to the effect that you were quite certain that there was no Prime Ministerial instruction for the Solicitor General's letter to be leaked.

In view of the comments of Members of the Defence Select Committee in Wednesday's debate on the tightly drafted and limited conclusion of the Select Committee in Par. 183, as to the extent of the Prime Minister's knowledge of the actions of her office, and confined to what was done on that day on her direct authority, have you any further information which you may wish to set out upon which your answer is based?

It may be that you would wish to give further consideration to your answer. If you still stand by it, may I presume that you are quite certain that the Prime Minister did not contemplate beforehand the leaking of the Solicitor General's letter, that is before 6 January.

The Sunday Telegraph article of 27 July under its headline 'Havers Threatens to call Police to No 10' has caused some anxiety to my colleagues. Should you wish to comment, it would help to clarify the position that you took and, in particular, I would be interested in knowing whether you had as alleged warned the Director of Public Prosecutions that police action might be necessary.

Yours ever
John

To the Rt Hon. John Morris QC, MP:
31 October 1986

Dear John

Thank you for your letter of today's date.

In my answer to Tam Dalyell on 14 July 1986 I was intending to express what was and is my opinion.

I do not want to add anything further.

Yours ever
Michael

Sir Michael, a man of normally equable temper, saw red when Sir Robert Armstrong began to make excuses as to why there should not be an inquiry. 'I have spoken to the Director of Public Prosecutions,' said the Attorney General, 'and I will have the police here if you do not immediately hold an inquiry.'[1]

Whitehall rumour has it that Sir Robert summoned the Prime Minister's private secretary Nigel Wicks, and told him to listen to the Attorney. I understand that Mr Wicks, a Whitehall high-flier, destined to become a Permanent Secretary, went pale as the Attorney revealed that he had already briefed a Chief Inspector of police, just in case Number Ten Downing Street did refuse to co-operate.

Incandescent with anger, the Prime Minister agreed to an inquiry. Had she not done so, the Attorney at that point in time would have resigned on a matter of principle,

---

[1] Reported by Adam Raphael in the *Observer*.

taking the Solicitor General with him. It would have been one thing to lose a Defence Secretary – another to lose a Trade Secretary – but to have the Law Officers resigning as well, on a matter of principle, would certainly have portended a change of Prime Minister, if not a change of Government.

If I appear to concentrate on the Solicitor General's letter, it may focus the searchlight on a fringe issue. To such a reaction there is a double riposte. First, the truthfulness or otherwise of the head of government is emphatically not a fringe issue. Secondly, Law Officers' letters are themselves of great importance. For, unlike a Ministerial letter, a Law Officer's letter can matter in the courts. That is why they are handled so gingerly in Government Departments.[1] Rows about Law Officers' letters are not what Mr Brian Redhead of the *Today* programme terms 'Westminster shenanigans'. The issue is the integrity of the British government.

On 7 January 1986, the headlines ranged from 'Heseltine told by Law Chief: Stick to the facts' in *The Times*, to 'You Liar!' in the *Sun*. If there had been a modicum of good faith in the actions of the Prime Minister, why was not one obvious thing done? A telephone call to the author of the letter, asking for his permission to publish it, would have sufficed. The snag about such a course is that Patrick Mayhew would have asked *why* it should be published – not to mention that he would also have objected in the most picturesque language to the notion that the letter be leaked selectively. Yet *selective* leaking constituted the whole purpose of the letter.

The position is set out in paragraph 35 of the October 1986 Government response to the Defence Committee's report:

[1] Historians and students of politics will remember that it was a Law Officer's letter in the Campbell case in 1924 which was the immediate cause of the fall of the first Labour Government.

The Committee say that they do not believe that the
authority of the Secretary of State for Trade and Industry
was sufficient to make public parts of a document which
contained the advice of a Law Officer without the knowledge or permission of the Law Officer. As the Committee make clear, there is a rule that it is not permissible,
save with the prior authority of the Law Officers, to
disclose to anybody outside the United Kingdom
Government service what advice the Law Officers have
given in a particular question or whether they have
given, or have been or may be asked to give, such
advice. In this case the prior authority of the Law Officer
concerned was not sought or given.

The unanswered question is: why was authority neither
sought nor given?

In paragraph 178 of the Select Committee Report, the
MPs refer to their question to Mr Brittan: 'Why was the
Solicitor General not told that his letter was going to be
leaked?' Mr Brittan, they recorded, would not tell them.
It was not until *Wednesday 22 January* that Patrick Mayhew
discovered that disclosure of parts of his letter had been
authorised by Leon Brittan. Mayhew confirmed that it was
on that Wednesday that he saw Sir Robert Armstrong's
report on the circumstances of the disclosure. This was an
outrageous way in which to treat any Minister. To make
matters worse, in a letter copied round Whitehall, Mayhew
had expressed his 'dismay that a letter containing confidential legal advice from a Law Officer to one of his
colleagues should have been leaked and leaked moreover
in a highly selective way'.

Apart from the fact that Mayhew and Heseltine were
old political friends, Mayhew knew that Heseltine's letter
was not necessarily wrong. Nor did he, as Law Officer,
even have the evidence to make a firm judgment one way
or the other. He felt he had been tricked into writing the
letter. The notion put around at the time, to the effect that
Mayhew had been quietly browsing over his Saturday

morning's *Times* and, reading about Westland, had suddenly jumped up and goaded himself into drafting a shirty letter to Heseltine, is far-fetched in the extreme. Some of us look forward to Patrick Mayhew's memoirs.

Henry the Second

The moment she saw her position on Westland threatened, and herself entering into a crunch situation, Mrs Thatcher began, characteristically, to misbehave as a Prime Minister.

When, on 4 January and 5 January 1986, she and her closest entourage in Number Ten Downing Street hit on the idea of discrediting their own Defence Secretary by suggesting to the Solicitor General that he write a letter making out that Mr Heseltine was wrong in law, there was no other purpose in the Prime Minister's mind than that the letter should be leaked. More culpable still, the letter, when it came from Patrick Mayhew, was couched in typically careful and sensible terms, and therefore had to be selectively leaked. The actual method was the use of Mr Chris Moncrieff of the Press Association, later described by Denzil Davies, the Shadow Defence Secretary, as 'the purveyor of information to the public domain'.

Thus the excuse for the selectivity of the leaking, to the effect that the letter had to be dictated over the telephone and therefore only extracts could be taken down in shorthand, is preposterous. Those of us who work with Chris Moncrieff know that he is among the most remarkable takers of shorthand in Britain, and that his news sense is second to none. He would instantly have understood the importance and likely consequences of the information he was being given.

And there is one other aspect of Mr Moncrieff's role, which may seem trivial and internal to Westminster, but which was as important to me as the Sethia diaries had been in the case of the *Belgrano*. It was the simple fact that this critical information came from Mr Moncrieff of all journalists. This meant to me that someone had approached him, because Mr Moncrieff is not an investig- ative journalist, going searching for stories and well- publicised personal by-lines. That is not his job, nor how he perceives his job. His job is to get information quickly and accurately on to the Press Association tapes. Further- more, Mr Moncrieff must have been satisfied that the 'someone' who approached him was in a position to know about a Law Officer's letter, otherwise never in a month of Sundays would he have put the story out. In other words, Mr Moncrieff must have known precisely to whom he was talking, and been satisfied of their state of knowl- edge about the letter. Equally, only a politician would approach, or give instructions to approach, Mr Moncrieff. No civil servant in their right mind would contact Mr Moncrieff without explicit Ministerial authority, albeit that Mr Moncrieff would rather go to the stake and fiery furnace than reveal a source.

Mr Brittan is in no doubt where the responsibility should lie. 'I would particularly stress, it all had to be subject to the agreement of No. 10,' he told the Select Committee. When the Prime Minister was challenged by the Shadow Attorney General, John Morris, who asked her in a letter if she had pre-planned the leak and whether she had set up an inquiry already knowing the circumstances of how it had occurred, Mrs Thatcher refused point-blank to reply, claiming that she had already given a full account. 'I have nothing to add,' she wrote. The Ministerial stone-wall has become an insult to Parliament. Equally, the Government White Paper, published in October 1986, is absolutely brazen in its approach. The nearest it gets to an apology is the following paragraph:

The Prime Minister, the then Secretary of State for Trade and Industry and the Head of the Home Civil Service have all expressed their regret that the Solicitor General's letter was disclosed in the way it was disclosed.

But the Government is satisfied that those concerned acted in good faith, and remains of the view that, having regard to all the circumstances, disciplinary proceedings were not called for.

I'm not for vengeance to be dished out to civil servants. But one is entitled to ask: Why not? The only explanation is that Ministers knew full well that politicians and not civil servants were to blame. For the Prime Minister's version of events is extraordinary. Mrs Thatcher is not just seeking to deny her own very considerable role in the leaking of a Law Officer's letter aimed at discrediting one of her Cabinet colleagues, but in addition is claiming that all concerned who committed a potentially criminal offence were 'acting in good faith'.

Contrast this approach with the Crichel Down case of four decades ago, often quoted as the textbook guide to ministerial conduct. The then Minister of Agriculture, Sir Thomas Dugdale, was at the centre of a political storm over compulsorily purchased land which his Department had mishandled without his knowledge. Although he had taken no direct part in the issue, Sir Thomas chose to resign. By modern standards, such a resignation may be thought to be taking things a bit far. But surely it is not too much to ask of Ministers that they should take the blame for actions which may have gone sour, but which they themselves initiated?

What really distinguishes the modern Tories from the old, or Mrs Thatcher from Mr Heath, is that they want above all to win. Winning has become an obsession. For this Prime Minister, and all those budding Ministers to whom she sets an example, scruples and integrity of behaviour simply clutter the path to victory.

The Prime Minister's role is best summed up by a former Cabinet colleague, a Conservative Privy Councillor whose name is known to me, quoted by Adam Raphael in the *Observer*: 'It is a perfectly simple story of straightforward dishonesty.'

It has been suggested by some that the Prime Minister should be protected by the doctrine of proportionality. This doctrine purports to hold that whatever blame might attach to Mrs Thatcher for the leak of the Solicitor General's letter, a Prime Ministerial resignation would be quite out of proportion.

But truth is truth is truth, and lies are lies are lies. If Trade Secretaries lay down their political careers, why is it disproportionate that the real culprit, the Prime Minister, be asked to do the same?

The stone-wall

It is over forty years since I first met Robert Armstrong. Head boy at Eton (where he was superbly taught in the Classics by the late Richard Martineau and the subsequent Headmaster of Rugby, Walter Hamilton) and scholar of Christ Church, Oxford, Sir Robert epitomises the pinnacle of verbal skill in the English language.

On a Wednesday afternoon, 5 February 1986, I sat in the Committee Room and reflected that Martineau and Hamilton would have been proud of their Eton handiwork. On Mrs Thatcher's instructions, the Cabinet Secretary had been hauled back from Honolulu where he was preparing economic meetings of importance to the United Kingdom – political embarrassment takes precedence over economic well-being any day – to appear before the Select Committee in lieu of other civil servants it wished to interview. He was judged to have the safest pair of hands.

But his appearance in reality proved to be a cul-de-sac not only for the Committee. It was also a cul-de-sac for the system of Parliamentary scrutiny of Government actions. Sir Robert hedged with an elegance which would have left the authors of *Yes, Minister* gasping for breath. It was the St John the Baptist performance before Australia and the Peter Wright case, where he was to present a phrase which will last for a thousand years, wherever

English is spoken. That day, his description of the leak of the Mayhew letter in a campaign designed to discredit a Cabinet Minister as 'regrettable' brought the memorable riposte from my colleague Dr John Gilbert, the MP for Dudley. 'You use language which would be appropriate to a waiter spilling soup in a restaurant.' But the truth, uncomfortable though it is for an MP to say it, is that my colleagues were outmanoeuvred. And for a very simple reason.

The House of Commons, unlike the American Congress, is not only a legislature. It is also Bagehot's 'pool of talent' from which the executive is chosen. An American Senator is not beholden to the White House for his promotion – he depends on the good opinion of others on Capitol Hill. And in the House of Commons, Select Committees, unlike those of Congress, have no control of financial purse strings. Worse still, the governing Party is always in the majority. Now, chairmen of Select Committees are usually ex-Ministers, or past Ministerial-aspirant seniority. But they may want to become Members of the House of Lords, or their wives might want to become peeresses. They want to keep their noses clean with their own Party.

Other members of the Select Committee may be ex-Ministers or no-hopefuls, but if Conservative, there will be pressure on them from their own areas to get the gong of knighthood. As one put it to me, at the end of the list for his intake, 'I'm a Quaker and don't really believe in these things – but if I didn't become a Sir, my Constituency Conservative Association would think I was a rogue!' Others still, on Select Committees, have Ministerial batons in their knapsacks and don't want to create offence. Therefore they are unlikely to insist on actions against their Government's wishes, let alone summon the head of Government.

I know at first hand. In 1967, in my innocence, I thought that as a Select Committee member of the Committee on Science and Technology, what better than to have Harold Wilson, as Prime Minister, along to explain his views on nuclear power?[1] The hornet's nest that descended on my unsuspecting head was unbelievable. The Government Chief Whip in a tizzy. That great libertarian, the diarist Dick Crossman, telling me in lurid language that I was acting above my station in life! So I know the power of patronage, and the pull of Party. But the fact is that the House of Commons funks interrogating its grandees as they should on occasion be interrogated.

Mrs Thatcher's key role in apparently inspiring the Mayhew letter in the first place, and then turning the Nelson eye as the leak took place, has never been denied. But it is also never likely to be admitted, precisely because it is in no one's interest in the Conservative Party that the issue should once again be raised.

Indeed, they made sure that it would be buried, by getting the chairman to agree that publication date would be at the fag-end of the session, the day after the Royal Wedding between Prince Andrew and Miss Sarah Ferguson. We should hardly be surprised. The same tactics had prevailed over the publication of the Foreign Affairs Select Committee Report on the *Belgrano*, which came out just as Parliament was off on its summer holidays.

There is, of course, also the question as to whether it is proper for any civil servant to be asked to wash politicians' dirty laundry, however elevated the authority for doing so. (This is a topic to which we will return when we look at the Wright case.) There is at least one heavyweight civil servant who is publicly appalled in the aftermath of the Westland leak. Sir Peter Middleton, permanent secretary at the Treasury, has told his officials to refuse to accept any instruction which compromises their political neutrality and constitutional integrity. Middleton has made it clear that he expects them to use procedures laid down by the Civil Service code of conduct which suggests that they seek the advice of their superiors, and if necessary the

[1] In retrospect, the idea is even more justified than it seemed to me at the time.

official head of the department, if they are faced with ethical or professional dilemmas.

In the case of the *Belgrano* papers Clive Ponting's difficulty was that his permanent secretary, Sir Clive Whitmore, had been Mrs Thatcher's most favourite of all civil servants during his time as Principal Private Secretary at Number Ten, and Ponting believed that he would have simply received a career-destroying raspberry to no purpose, if he had gone to Sir Clive and said, 'Please, sir, HMG are behaving badly towards that dreadful Tam Dalyell!'[1] I also thought it egregious of Sir Robert Armstrong to suggest that Ponting should have gone to knock on his door if he was dissatisfied at what he was being asked to do.[2]

The only real solution is to set up a body of senior persons to whom dissatisfied servicemen, civil servants, police officers and the like can go. This is the substance of the Cirencester and Tewkesbury amendment, passed by the 1985 Labour Party Conference at Bournemouth – some call it a 'Charter for Deep-throats'. Yet without information, campaigners for the truth are at a hopeless disadvantage.

It is one of the more curious aspects of Westland, much commented on in the Civil Service, that Sir Robert Armstrong, for all his insistence on correct form, has refused to discipline any of the civil servants directly involved. The conclusion is widely accepted that the only reason for not disciplining them is that the Cabinet Secretary knows full well that it was not more junior civil servants, but politicians who were guilty.

[1] For the full account of the sequence of events leading up to Clive Ponting's decision to send me the *Belgrano* information, see pp. 125–54 of his book *The Right to Know* (Sphere Books, 1985).

[2] As egregious as the Foreign Affairs Committee's decision to hand the documentation back to Michael Heseltine after I had placed them in its care: another example of the weak-minded behaviour characteristic of Select Committees.

A character about his Lady's business

Mr Bernard Ingham is no mere Press Secretary. He is, arguably, the most important *man* in the British Government. His role in the Westland affair – albeit a civil servant, paid for by the taxpayer – was to obscure the Prime Minister's responsibility for what took place. In her statements to the House of Commons on 23 and 27 January, Mrs Thatcher acknowledged that her private office had acted in accordance with her wish that the Solicitor General's letter 'should become public knowledge as soon as possible'. Yet she also repeatedly disclaimed any responsibility for the form of the leak and has refused to clarify when she was told what had been done in her name. The reader may get a taste about the Prime Minister's response to questions about the involvement of her office from the following exchange of 23 January 1986, reproduced as paragraph 198 in the report of the Defence Select Committee:

Mr Tam Dalyell (Linlithgow): 'When did the Prime Minister's press office first tell her what it had done?'

The Prime Minister: 'I have given as full an account – [interruption] – of the inquiry that I established to establish the facts. I have said that I was not consulted at the time.'

Mr Max Madden (Bradford, West): . . . 'When was she told by her officials of their involvement in the agreement to disclose the Solicitor-General's letter by the Department of Trade and Industry?'

The Prime Minister: 'A vast number of the facts in that report were not given to me until yesterday. I am not going to tease out what was and what was not. A number of the facts which came in that report were not known to me until yesterday.'

Mr George Foulkes (Carrick, Cumnock and Doon Valley): 'Will the Prime Minister give the House an assurance now that when she has "teased out" the details, as she describes them, she will tell the House exactly when she was told of her officers' involvement in the disclosure?'

The Prime Minister: 'I set up an inquiry to find out the facts. I discovered most of the facts when the inquiry had been reported.'

In replying in this way, and further in apportioning blame to 'misunderstandings' between civil servants, this Prime Servant is unceremoniously rubbishing a crucial convention of the British constitution: Ministerial responsibility. Mayhew wrote to the Defence Secretary, as we have seen, on 6 January 1986. It is clear, as the All-Party Select Committee on Defence found, that the Prime Minister had instigated the letter, and did so with a view to its being published. The letter was ultimately leaked, by the Department of Trade and Industry. It has been admitted under pressure by the Prime Minister that Number Ten knew of the leak and, as Sir Robert Armstrong said, 'accepted it'.[1]

The point that has been missed too often is that Sir Robert Armstrong's is a fundamental admission with direct consequences for Mrs Thatcher. To protect her, Government sources, orchestrated by Mr Ingham, continuously stressed that the leak was by the Department of Trade and Industry, not Number Ten, and that Number Ten never 'approved' the leak. But this assertion, in any event highly questionable, is a diversion. The Department of Trade and Industry was simply the means of distribution for the leak. It was a subordinate Ministry to the Prime Minister's Office. The duty of Mr Ingham and other civil servants in Number Ten, in such circumstances, was surely not simply to be indifferent to the leak, but actively to oppose it, and to say, 'No, you don't leak, and you certainly don't leak selectively.'

[1] This coincides exactly with what was said by officials of the Department of Trade and Industry for all to hear at the dinner for the Turkish Minister of Technology, Mustaffa Titiz, on 30 January 1986.

If this was the duty of the Prime Minister's Office, then it is quite impossible to see how the Prime Minister herself is not liable for the acts of her officials in accordance with the doctrine of Ministerial responsibility. Certainly, the doctrine of Ministerial responsibility lacks firm definition. But where a Minister instructs officials to secure an objective, and a senior official then does precisely that, but in a way that is improper, it is difficult to see how that doctrine can fail to apply.

In the context of public life in Britain, I believe the doctrine of Ministerial responsibility to be paramount. How else do we ensure that civil servants are protected from being made liable for carrying out their orders? How else do we ensure that Ministers are accountable to Parliament for the acts of their Departments?

The natural consequences of a Minister shirking responsibility is that the civil servant himself or herself becomes responsible. Yet perhaps one of the most extraordinary elements of the whole Westland affair is the absence of any punishment or any disciplinary proceedings against anyone, Ministers or civil servants. Yes, Leon Brittan went – but not because he or his officials had behaved improperly, because he had 'lost the confidence of his colleagues'. What is the explanation of Mr Ingham continuing to bask in Prime Ministerial favour, or Mr Charles Powell and Mr John Mogg to rise and rise in the Whitehall firmament?[1] Had they been to blame, should they have not gone the way of Tisdall and Ponting? There is something particularly unpleasant about attacking civil servants when they have tried to be honest with the elected Parliament, but then harbouring them, with the impression that they are at fault, when the real mischief is the work of politicians for highly political purposes.

It was also simply inappropriate for Mr Ingham, on his

[1] Charles Powell is Private Secretary to the Prime Minister (Overseas Affairs), and John Mogg, previously Principal Private Secretary to Leon Brittan, is now Under-Secretary of the European Commercial and Industrial Policy Division at the DTI.

own initiative, to offer 'cover' – whatever that may mean – for selectively leaking a Law Officer's letter. What sort of position can Mr Ingham have imagined that he was putting Miss Colette Bowe into, when he required her to phone up Mr Chris Moncrieff with selective contents of that letter? I cannot imagine Sir Donald Maitland, Ted Heath's press secretary, or the late William Clarke, or Joe Haines or Sir Tom McCaffrey or any other holder of the important office of press secretary, deeming it proper or ethical to make any such request of a civil servant colleague. At the very least, before contemplating anything of the kind, a person in this position would seek a Prime Ministerial instruction.

During his Suntory Toyota lecture, Sir Frank Cooper, Permanent Secretary at the Ministry of Defence during the Falklands War, went further:

A further paradox is that the more it has become technically easier to communicate, the less good has that communication become between Government and the governed. Indeed, the aim now is the management of the media with a very much higher degree of central control from Number 10 Downing Street and with the connivance of a part of the media. There is now public relations – which I would define as biased information. I suggest that the post of Chief Information officer at Number 10 Downing Street is in fact a political job in a Party sense and is not a job which it is proper for a civil servant to fill unless he, or she, resigns from the Civil Service on appointment. Moreover, what is said ought to be said on the record. The participation of the media in the lobby system is a public disgrace.

The non-appearance of Mr Ingham before a Select Committee of the House of Commons is a travesty of Parliamentary procedure. In the folklore of Westminster, it is said that one of the most awesome sights that a member of the public may see is one Miss Mary Frampton, a formidable official who works in the office of the Sergeant at Arms. As should be known to students of the constitution, Select Committees of the Commons have unconstrained powers to call for persons and papers. The late Dick Crossman, whose Parliamentary Private Secretary I was between 1964 and 1970, thought that this was the most effective weapon a Leader of the House of Commons could bestow on these inquisitorial committees. No less a personage than Arthur Scargill in his heyday was once confronted by Miss Frampton after his initial refusal to come to a Select Committee on Trade and Industry. *Mirabile dictu*, Mr Scargill attended. Yet in the case of the Prime Minister's refusal to allow the key civil servants at the centre of the Westland Affair to appear before the Defence Select Committee, it was not so much a case of Miss Frampton turning up on the doorstep of Downing Street as of a reluctance on the part of the Conservative-dominated Select Committee to send her.

We are thus in the process of having a new political doctrine formed under our unwritten and flexible constitution: namely, that the previously untrammelled power to call any persons or papers should be trammelled to the extent that Ministers should be able to block the appearance of their civil servants before any hearings.

It may be conceded that the theory behind the Government's contention is impeccable. Ministers, not civil servants, are responsible to Parliament. Civil servants answer, and are responsible to, Ministers. Ministers should therefore answer for their actions to Commons Select Committees. The practice is a bit different. Civil servants have been appearing before Commons Select Committees for years. In so doing they have not been making policy, but indicating to my Parliamentary colleagues the manner in which they have carried out their decisions, given to them by Ministers to implement.

In an ever more complex world, where it is accepted that much power has inevitably devolved on civil servants, and in which it is physically impossible for Ministers to keep track of everything happening in their Departments, such a development is sensible. The problem with the Government's deployment of logic in the Westland case is that it does not follow it through. Why does it wish to stop civil servants appearing on this most sensitive of issues? In theory, the Government says in its response to the criticisms levelled at it in the Defence Select Committee Report that 'Ministers are responsible and accountable to their Departments in pursuit of Government policies or in the discharge of responsibilities laid upon them by Parliament'. In the event, none of the key Ministers involved has followed this dictum (Leon Brittan was out of office when he appeared), least of all the Prime Minister, over the issue of accepting responsibility for the authorisation of the leaking of the Mayhew letter.

The Prime Minister has rested on the unsatisfactory defence that the apparent authorisation went ahead 'without my direct authority'. She has in general stonewalled by declaring her faith in her key officials and protecting them by blocking their appearance before the Select Committee. Yet to any reasonable person, the words 'without my direct authority' suggest that the instructions Mrs Thatcher conveyed to Mr Ingham and other henchmen were a great deal clearer than those given by Henry Plantagenet, II of England, to those knights who rushed off to Canterbury to do away with St Thomas à Becket on his own altar. As we shall see later, it is the same style of government as: 'Who will rid me of this turbulent Duncan Campbell and all those programmes on *The Secret Society* that he is making for the BBC?'

So truth has been falsified to hide where the responsibility lies. Mrs Thatcher, thanks to the loyalty of her personal staff, her colleagues, and above all Mr Ingham, has survived. But her reputation for straight dealing has again been sullied. In being loyal to Mr Ingham, she is being loyal to the man who 'under orders' refused to give evidence to the Select Committee – whose orders does Mr Ingham take other than hers? – and is criticised for his central role in masterminding the leak of the Mayhew letter. *Any normal civil servant* who masterminded a leak of a Law Officer's letter would be dismissed forthwith.

The Prime Minister has always claimed that her officials acted without her knowledge, and that she did not know the full circumstances of how the leak had occurred until nearly a fortnight after it had taken place. Anybody looking at the Select Committee Report would have to regard this as a fairy tale. Mr Ingham's office is within shouting distance, and he sees his Prime Minister several times a day. How do we stretch our credulity to believe that they did not mention to each other the matter that was first on every news headline, rocking the very foundations of her Government? Mr Attlee may have stuck to *The Times* crossword, the cricket scores, and the births, marriages and deaths column, and retorted to a colleague who pointed out to him press criticism of him, 'Is that so? Circulation falling?' – but not Mrs Thatcher, who takes a Wilsonian interest in what the papers say.

The answer is that after 6 January 1986 there probably was no need for consultation with the Prime Minister. Mr Ingham and Mr Powell knew precisely what they had to do before ever the innocent Solicitor General was set up to put pen to paper. It is really very simple – if Mr Ingham and his Civil Service colleagues were not carrying out her orders, then they should at least be removed from their posts, if not punished. If the Prime Minister is not prepared to punish them, then she should admit the truth, and confess that they were indeed carrying out her orders.

Another lacuna in the whole tale is the role of Mr Nigel Wicks, the Principal Private Secretary, a position always held by one of the brightest members of his Civil Service generation. Even if, from 7 January onwards, the Prime Minister was content to leave the matter to others, it is a cause for astonishment that Mr Wicks did not make immediate enquiries into a matter which appeared to involve a member of the Private Office – Mr Charles Powell – which he headed. The only explanation is that

Mr Wicks, like Mr Ingham and Mr Powell, knew what was up and wished to distance the Prime Minister from the consequences.

Mr Ingham and Mr Powell are not just ordinary civil servants. The Prime Minister would see far more of them than either the Cabinet Secretary, or her Cabinet colleagues. They were as close to Mrs Thatcher as Robert Haldemann and John Ehrlichmann were to Richard Nixon.

An innocent bystander

The perceptive then political editor of the *Observer*, Adam Raphael, began one of many memorable articles thus: 'WHAT BLUNT BERNARD SAID TO RELUCTANT COLETTE.' Under the headline, Raphael wrote: '"You will *** do as you are *** well told." With these blunt expletives, the Prime Minister's Press Secretary, Bernard Ingham, touched off the Westland Affair.' The phraseology has never been denied, and I know that Mr Raphael, from other sources, is correct. The instructions were directed by Bernard Ingham at the Chief Information Officer at the Department of Trade and Industry, Miss Colette Bowe. Her qualms about leaking the Solicitor General's letter were the first hurdle to be jumped by Mr Ingham in his campaign to discredit Michael Heseltine without leaving any fingerprints.

Being a receptacle for information, I had it vouchsafed to me that not only had Colette Bowe been the instrument of the selective leak to Chris Moncrieff, but that she herself had done it only because she was acting, not merely on Ministerial instructions, but on Prime Ministerial instructions. Otherwise, nothing would have induced me to name an individual civil servant of comparable rank in the House of Commons. We now learn that Miss Bowe, along with at least one of her colleagues, has placed her version of events in a bank vault – not exactly the action of a civil servant who accepted the version of events put out by the

Government as being in accord with her own recollection.

As a career civil servant, Miss Bowe was placed in an impossible situation. She did try to contact the permanent secretary, Sir Brian Hayes, not least because she wondered why it could be that giving extracts from the Mayhew letter to the Press Association was 'the only way to do it in time'? Mrs Thatcher was to tell us in the House of Commons that 'it was especially important in this situation for statements made on behalf of the Government, on which commercial judgments might be based, to be accurate and in no way misleading. That being so, it was a matter of duty that it should be made known publicly that there were thought to be material inaccuracies which needed to be corrected in Mr Heseltine's letter.' The deadline which everyone seemed to be fussing about was 4 p.m. that day, 6 January, when the Westland press conference was due to begin. It was Westland themselves who had first drawn attention to differences between Mr Heseltine's letter of 3 January to Lloyds Merchant Bank and the Prime Minister's letter of 1 January to Sir John Cuckney. Sir John Cuckney, chairman of Westland, had said to an official of the DTI on 5 January that it was very important to the company that the discrepancies should be cleared up before the press conference the next day which was to rally shareholders behind the Sikorsky bid.

Yet the information was given first, *not* to the company, but to the Press Association. Why? Simply to discredit Michael Heseltine – and that Miss Bowe did not approve of, not least because she had been involved as a civil servant with Mr Heseltine when he was Environment Secretary, trying to do something on Merseyside.

From the passages chosen for selective disclosure, it is perfectly clear that the Solicitor General's letter was calculated to do the maximum damage to Mr Heseltine's case and to his personal credibility. This is not only my opinion but that of the All-Party Select Committee.[1] But

[1] Paragraph 162, Defence Select Committee Report HC519.

an examination of the Press Association tapes on 6 January, and the reports carried by newspapers on 7 January, reveals that further parts of the letter were disclosed after the original call from Miss Bowe to the Press Association. Any urgency argument, to get the message to the Westland board, could not apply to these disclosures. Their only purpose can have been further to discredit Mr Heseltine. The fact that additional disclosures appear to have been made has not been acknowledged by the Government.

The deliberate leak was so open, so outrageous and so unconstitutional that Mayhew demanded that an official inquiry be set up. But on 16 January 1986 Sir Michael Havers, for whom Mayhew had deputised in writing the letter, returned from his sickbed and guaranteed Colette Bowe immunity from prosecution. According to paragraph 195 of the Select Committee's Report, 'the Attorney General said that when he was asked to grant immunity he was told enough "to make it clear to me that in no circumstances would I have prosecuted [Miss Bowe] in any event." These statements are unequivocal.' The Select Committee Report continues: 'Unauthorised disclosure would have been an offence. If "under no circumstances" would the Attorney General have prosecuted Miss Bowe, then he must have known that the disclosure had been authorised. He must also have received this information from Sir Robert Armstrong.' Prior to the Select Committee's Report, I thought that there could have been only one of two explanations for the Attorney's conduct. Either that he was deliberately misled by senior colleagues who asked for Miss Bowe's immunity while withholding from him the fact that the disclosure in question had been authorised. Or that Sir Michael Havers himself had participated in the charade of putting the spotlight on officials by being party to concealing the roles played in the leaking of the letter by Leon Brittan. Now, one of the ludicrous and astonishing facts about the Westland affair is that no Law Officer has been allowed to participate in a full debate. (This is partly the fault of the Shadow Cabinet, who insisted on putting up their members, rather than the Shadow Attorney General.) In answers to Parliamentary Questions the Attorney General has not fully explained why he gave immunity to Miss Bowe. He says that 'she acted in complete good faith'. But how can a breach of the Official Secrets Act be in complete good faith unless it is sanctioned by a Minister? Ask Sarah Tisdall or Clive Ponting about that.

Miss Bowe had been forced into an awkward position by Bernard Ingham, and I had a terrible, sleepless night about having named her. But she acted very sensibly and correctly from her own point of view. She asked for immunity from prosecution. She disapproved strongly of the action she had been forced to take, and was determined not to be made the scapegoat. Sir Robert Armstrong and Sir Michael Havers agreed. As Sir Robert put it, 'I believed I should be addressing [in my inquiry] the person who had actually passed the information. It was evident that a truthful answer could be an incriminating answer, and it seemed therefore likely to me that the person concerned might wish to know what the position would be in the event of a truthful answer being given. I therefore discussed the matter with Sir Michael Havers on, as you might say, a contingency basis, having reason to believe that I should be asked what the position was. Sure enough, I was asked what the position was [by Colette Bowe].'

Now the granting of immunity in such a situation, if there was ever the like, is quite extraordinary. Sauce for the goose and sauce for the gander: in the case of the *Belgrano* papers the Ministry of Defence police were called in right away, since charges under the Official Secrets Act might – and did – result. Why did not the same thing happen on 6 and 7 January?

The whole investigation was an ugly farce. Sir Robert Armstrong conducted an inquiry, but he was not authorised to interview the Ministers who had the responsibility for authorising the leak in the first place. If he had been, his inquiry would have rapidly petered out since, as the Cabinet Secretary himself pointed out later, a leak that is authorised by a Minister is no leak at all.

The under-footman

We cannot leave the Westland affair without a few words about George Younger. In wholly unexpected circumstances, the long-serving Secretary of State for Scotland was offered the job which he had always craved (Secretary of State for Defence), but had given up hope of getting. His strategy over Westland was to consign it to history, perhaps to be picked over by constitutional experts and learned academics. Neatly packaged, it will all be shoved away for at least thirty years when some extra light might be shed on the events of January 1986 in confidential records and papers. During the debate on the Select Committee Report, Mr Younger devoted all of three minutes to the fundamental question which was exercising his fellow MPs – the truthfulness or otherwise of his Prime Minister. To paraphrase Senator Howard Baker's famous question to Richard Nixon over Watergate: What did she know and when did she know it? Mr Younger simply used every device to allow time and memory to obscure the original offence with which the Government was charged, and doubtless he will go on doing so.

Like some other Cabinet Ministers, George Younger took the cynical view that Westland was never seen as a matter which aroused great public passions, and it was from that assessment that their collective sigh of relief came.

Ministers' response to the Defence Select Committee Report showed a remarkable degree of complacency, if not of wilful misunderstanding. Its main conclusion was that the Government will instruct civil servants, appearing before such committees, not to answer questions about their own conduct, or that of named colleagues. This reinforces the principle (challenged in the Ponting trial) that civil servants are responsible only to their Ministers. But this principle only works if the latter accept the responsibility which they in turn owe to Parliament. It was because Ministers acted in contradiction to that rule in 1986 that officials have found themselves taking the flak for political decisions. The Government's latest proposals and rulings will not reduce the vulnerability of civil servants in such circumstances unless Ministers fulfil their part of the bargain. Since, by the nature of the business, there can be no guarantee of that – under any Government – a code of ethics seems a useful means of disciplining both politicians and bureaucrats into behaving in accordance with the constitutional convention. George Younger has many virtues, but I doubt, from experience of him as a Minister in Scotland since 1970, whether zeal for the reform needed to prevent a re-run of Westland is one of them.

Is it really worth raking over the sorry story of the Westland company, in the light of the success politicians and subsequent events have had in drawing it from the public's mind? There is a forceful parallel to be drawn between the events of December 1985 and January 1986, and the scandal which emerged last year in the United States over the illegal supply of arms to the Contra rebels in Nicaragua. 'Irangate' and Westland may be different in scale, and vastly so, but the central questions in both cases are the same ones: *was the head of Government involved in acts of dishonesty, and were those acts covered up?* The Americans have instinctively understood that this issue strikes at the heart of government. We have not. Instead of accumulating evidence, we have accumulated indifference. But if we allow the truth about Westland to hide in a dark corner, how can we expect truth to be the touchstone of our Government's, and our Prime Minister's, other activity?

3

Libyan Roulette

The House of Commons can be like a flight of starlings. We move on from one perch to another. A chorus of opinion expresses itself on the issue of today, and yesterday's issue is all but forgotten. For my part, I am an unashamed yesterday's-issue politician, who thinks Parliament moves on far too fast, and has an unhealthily developed forgettory. The moment the American bombs had burst over Tripoli and Benghazi, Mrs Thatcher could know that she was sailing away from the shoals of danger of the Westland affair. MPs were understandably engrossed in a momentous event.

One day, some historian or investigative reporter, with access to Federal Washington and perhaps interviews with ex-President Reagan, will write an authoritative account of an action which could have conceivably led to a superpower crisis and which will, I believe, have an indelible effect on the perception people in the Arab world have of the West. For the present, however, all I can usefully do is to present the reader with a very personal account of what was globally the most serious potential crisis with which this book deals, or in which Mrs Thatcher has been involved since she became Prime Minister.

About 10 p.m. in the evening of 14 April 1986, I received one of the familiar pink slips in the Members' Lobby of the House of Commons, requesting me urgently to return a call. It came from some members of Stroud Constituency

Labour Party in Gloucestershire, people who had been
friends ever since I had been to a meeting they organised
in Stroud Town Hall the previous year. Somewhat agitat-
edly my friends told me that there had been a massive
take-off of American planes from the base at Upper
Heyford which some of their members monitored round
the clock, and also, they believed, from the airfield at
Fairford. Might the United States have moved on from
sabre-rattling about Middle East terrorism and initiated a
strike on Libya?

I did not dismiss the suggestion, and wondered whether
I should storm into the House, and on a necessarily bogus
'point of order' make a fuss on the Floor of the House. I
decided against. First of all, I had no hard knowledge,
only speculation, that Libya was indeed the ultimate
destination; secondly, I could not really believe that the
Americans would strike at Libya; and thirdly, why should
they strike from Britain when they had the formidable
Sixth Fleet lying in the Gulf of Sirte? Finally, I am an
exceedingly cautious man, sensitive to the fact that so
many of my non-Labour Parliamentary colleagues would
like to see me slip on a spectacular banana skin, so that
they could discredit everything and anything else I might
say. I simply was not on certain enough ground, even to
interrupt the proceedings and ask some questions.

There was too another consideration, in the form of the
nature of Commons business that evening. It was the
contentious debate on Sunday trading, and it was about
the only time in the life of this Parliament when there was
the risk of defeat on a major Government proposal. I was
very loth to incur the ire of Labour friends by getting
Conservative backs up on another subject, when some of
those Conservatives were steeling themselves to join the
Labour Party in the Opposition Lobbies against their own
Government's Sunday trading proposals. In the Chamber
I have become like a red rag to a bull for many Tory MPs
(though my relations outside the Chamber are perfectly
decent at a human level).

Out of such domestic trivia come decisions. To my dying day, I shall wonder what would have happened if the business had been more interruptible, and I had been a little less cautious. Had I interrupted the Commons, the nature of the interruption might have been on the Press Association tapes (as Mr Chris Moncrieff or Mr Tom McMullan would have contacted my sources in Gloucestershire), and had the PA covered the issue, it might have got through to the Libyans that American planes were at that moment winging their way from Britain to strike at targets in their country. Had the Libyans had this intelligence, would the Americans have lost planes? Would the scheme, the element of surprise lost, have been aborted? How might history have been changed?

At 1 a.m. on 15 April I walked back to my room near the House and slumped into bed, pleased that the Government had been defeated and that the Sabbath in England – if not Scotland – was safe for a decade.

On the 6.30 news, as I was shaving in the dawn of 15 April, there came the stunning tidings of the American attack on Libya, the numbing accompanying information that our country was deeply involved, and the horrendous realisation that maybe I should have acted differently the night before, and gone on making a real nuisance of myself in the House until the tapes confirmed for my colleagues the information that had come from the Gloucestershire Labour Parties. I really had butterflies in the stomach as to what would happen next. So ill-conceived did they imagine President Reagan's operation to be that France, Spain, Portugal and Italy would not even permit over-flying rights for the UK-based American aircraft. Alone in Europe, Mrs Thatcher's Britain had entered into complicity with the Americans.

When, at 3.31 p.m. that day, the Prime Minister rose in her place to make a statement, it was the most sombre moment in the House of Commons since the loss of HMS *Sheffield* during the Falklands War. And, frankly, feelings were cross-party. In candour, quite a number of Labour

MPs thought Colonel Gadaffi had got what he deserved, and a number of Conservative Arabists were profoundly unhappy at the madness (as they saw it) of offending the entire Arab world, even those who entertained little affection for the Libyan regime.

If I print the Prime Minister's statement in full, it is partly because I must not be guilty of the selectivity about which I complained in the last chapter, and partly because it was not only the basis for HMG's position during the crisis, but has remained the basis for justification of the Government's action:

The Prime Minister: With permission, Mr Speaker, I shall make a statement about Libya. Before I do so, may I first say that my right hon. Friend the Leader of the House, will shortly be making a business statement indicating that there will be a full day's debate on this matter tomorrow.

The House is aware that last night United States forces made attacks on specific targets in Libya.

The Government have evidence showing beyond dispute that the Libyan Government have been and are directly involved in promoting terrorist attacks against the United States and other Western countries, and that they had made plans for a wide range of further terrorist attacks.

The United Kingdom has itself suffered from Libyan terrorism. The House will recall the murder of WPC Fletcher in St James's Square. There is no doubt, moreover, of the Libyan Government's direct and continuing support for the provisional IRA, in the form of money and weapons.

Two years ago, we took certain measures against Libya, including the closure of the Libyan people's bureau in London, restrictions on the entry of Libyans into the United Kingdom, and a ban on new contracts for the export to Libya of defence equipment. Yesterday the Foreign Ministers of the European Community reaffirmed their grave concern at Libyan-inspired terrorism and agreed on new restrictions against Libya.

Since we broke off diplomatic relations with Libya, we have had no choice but consistently to advise British nationals living and working there that they do so on their own responsibility. Our interests there have been looked after by the Italian Government. Our representative in the British interests section of the Italian Embassy will continue to advise the British community as best he can.

The United States has tried by peaceful means to deter Colonel Gadaffi and his regime from their promotion of terrorism, but to no effect.

President Reagan informed me last week that the United States intended to take military action to deter further Libyan terrorism. He sought British support for this action. He also sought agreement, in accordance with our long-standing arrangements, to the use in the operation of some United States aircraft based in this country. This approach led to a series of exchanges including a visit by Ambassador Walters on Saturday, 12 April.

Article 51 of the UN charter specifically recognises the right to self-defence. In view of Libya's promotion of terrorism, the failure of peaceful means to deter it and the evidence that further attacks were threatened, I replied to the President that we would support action directed against specific Libyan targets demonstrably involved in the conduct and support of terrorist activities; and, further, that if the President concluded that it was necessary, we would agree to the deployment of United States aircraft from bases in the United Kingdom for that purpose.

I reserved the position of the United Kingdom on any question of further action which might be more general or less clearly directed against terrorism.

The President assured me that the operation would be limited to clearly defined targets related to terrorism,

and that the risk of collateral damage would be minimised. He made it clear that use of F1-11 aircraft from
bases in the United Kingdom was essential, because by
virtue of their special characteristics they would provide
the safest means of achieving particular objectives with
the lowest possible risk both of civilian casualties in
Libya and of casualties among United States service
personnel.

Terrorism is a scourge of the modern age. Libya has
been behind much of it and was planning more. The
United Kingdom itself has suffered from Libya's actions.
So have many of our friends, including several in the
Arab world.

The United States, after trying other means, has now
sought by limited military action to induce the Libyan
regime to desist from terrorism. That is in the British
interest. It is why the Government support the United
States action.

As soon as I heard it, I thought the statement was
flawed.

As I explained in the introduction, I am one of the few
people in the House of Commons who has a vast camel's
hump of technical knowledge (although there are whole
areas, such as immigration, housing policy and local
government, where I never open my mouth). Just as in
the case of Aldabra Atoll and my residual knowledge
about the nature of coral limestone being unfit as a runway
foundation, so my alarm bells rang as the Prime Minister
sat down. Hang on, I thought. What's this about the
risk of collateral damage being minimised? What's Mrs
Thatcher telling us – that she did it on humanitarian
grounds? What were the special characteristics in F1-11s
that would provide the best means of saving civilian casualties? Did I not remember somewhere in my mental locker
that Secretary of the Navy Lehmann had claimed that
his A6s – carrier-based aircraft – had the TAM tracking
equipment which made them the most accurate attack

aircraft on the planet? And was there not an aircraft carrier in the Gulf of Sirte?

Having been weekly columnist of *New Scientist* for over twenty years, I am in constant mental training as to 'fact' – a discipline to which most MPs are frankly not subjected. If I put a foot wrong, the Editor tends to receive a letter of usually gentle rebuke from some Fellow of the Royal Society or distinguished reader.

I smelt a rat in the Prime Minister's statement. Leaving the Chamber, I used unprintable language to my male MP colleagues about the Prime Minister's 'humanitarian' explanation of the granting of permission. Besides, what she had said was an implied insult to the capacity of the US Sixth Fleet. If they were not capable of doing that job on Tripoli and Benghazi by themselves, what on earth would they do if it were not the Libyans but the Soviet Union . . .

Mrs Thatcher contended that she had been acting on humanitarian grounds. For public consumption by an uneasy British audience, containment of killing became her justification. Yet from the Pentagon came very different reasons. First, the attack on Libya provided a proving ground for weapons. *US News and World Report* carried an article by William Broyles Jr on 12 May 1986 entitled 'The Politics of War', in which he writes, 'The budget, in short, is the mission. "It all comes back to the budget," says one ex-Pentagon analyst. "For years we've been saying that radar, infra-red, and smart bombs are the way to go. We've spent billions on night-mission avionics, so we had to try to use them, even if a daylight strike would have been better."' Equally bluntly, *Aviation Week* of 21 April asserted that the attack on Libya 'provided a good proving ground for the F1-11s to be flown in the Mediterranean, and gave the Air Force a chance to demonstrate its capabilities'. And it is simply not true that the bomb-aiming equipment on the F1-11s was superior to the carrier-borne A6s and A7s. They both had the TAM system or its equivalent.

A raid of this kind was deemed to have great value in the presentation to Congress of the case for greater spending on the US Navy and US Air Force.

But it was not a reason given by our Prime Minister to our House of Commons.

Secondly, there was inter-service rivalry involved, between the US Navy and US Air Force. As a senior official of the Pentagon artlessly put it to *Aviation Week*, '"Understandably, after the all-Navy action in Libya last month, the Air Force wanted a piece of the action."'

Again, this was not a reason given by our Prime Minister to our House of Commons, for the use of our territory in Britain as a base for non-NATO operations.

Thirdly, there has been the formidable lobby in the Pentagon which has been championing the idea of joint-service operations, particularly the use of land-based aircraft in support of naval operations.

When the joint chiefs of staff sat down in Washington in December 1985 to consider the military options against Libya, Admiral James Watkins – Chief of Naval Operations – and others saw a useful opportunity for a joint naval–air force operation to demonstrate the value of their concept to doubters in Congress and the Pentagon.

Again, this was not a reason hinted at by our Prime Minister to our House of Commons.

Fourthly, and possibly most important of all from the point of view of the House of Commons, whereas the internal politics of the US military were an important reason for the attacks on Libya, the nature and timing of the raid had much wider political implications. In the April 1986 issue of *Sanity*, Rear Admiral Eugene Carroll Jr, of the Center for Defense Information in Washington, was asked if, in his experience, it would have been practical to use the F1-11s, and ask the British afterwards. 'That was the basis,' said Carroll, 'on which the plan was prepared.' The implications are chilling.

Challenged as to her motives for allowing the use of British bases, Mrs Thatcher then switched to another line.

In her most scolding manner, she told me in the House that I ought to understand that hundreds of thousands of American troops were defending us in Europe and that one of them had been killed by Libyans at a West Berlin nightclub. Therefore it followed that permission for the use of Upper Heyford, Mildenhall, and Lakenheath for non-NATO purposes was justified.

First of all, there is the doctrine of proportionality. Could it be justified to launch a major attack simply in revenge for the killing, however awful, of one individual serviceman?

Secondly, it has transpired that it was most unlikely that it was the Libyans who were the perpetrators of the Berlin crime. I reproduce a timetable that Dr Richard Ware and Christopher Bowlby, impartial scholars of the House of Commons Library, have prepared:

Progress of investigations into responsibility for bomb at La Belle discotheque in Berlin on 5 April 1986

29 March 1986	Bomb at German–Arab Friendship Society in Berlin.
5 April 1986	Bomb at La Belle discotheque in Berlin.
5–14 April 1986	Reports and speculation centre on probability of Libyan involvement in La Belle attack; reports that police are looking for Libyan suspects; expulsion of Libyan diplomats (9 April), etc.
14–15 April 1986	US raid on Tripoli. President Reagan asserts 'irrefutable' evidence of Libyan connection with terrorism and refers to intercepted messages between Tripoli and Libyan People's Bureau in Berlin: 'The evidence is now con-

clusive that the terrorist bombing of La Belle discotheque was planned and executed under the direct orders of the Libyan regime.'

17 April 1986   Bomb attack on El Al plane foiled at Heathrow airport.

18 April 1986   Arrest in London of Nezar Hindawi in connection with El Al attempted bombing; Ahmed Hasi arrested in Berlin on suspicion of involvement in La Belle attack.

21 April 1986   US spokesman Larry Speakes quoted as saying that the arrest of Hasi, a Palestinian, in no way changed the 'conclusive evidence' that Libyans were involved in the La Belle attack. Later in the day it is revealed that Nezar Hindawi and Ahmed Hasi are brothers.

Der Spiegel quotes Berlin state security chief Manfred Ganshow's statement to a *Bundestag* home affairs committee that the Libyan connection is still only one important lead amongst several.

Christian Lochte, head of the Hamburg *Verfassungsschutz*, is quoted as saying that there is as yet 'no concrete evidence' of Libyan responsibility.

The explosion has apparently destroyed all traces of evidence for US and local investigators. Local criminal police are investigating 'in all possible directions', including the theory that rival disco-owners or drug dealers might have had a motive for the attack on La Belle.

23 April 1986

Volker Kühne, spokesman for the West Berlin Justice Department, says: 'We went to Hasi's house because of a tip from London, but he was arrested because of documents found at this house that raised the suspicion he was involved in the discotheque bombing' (Associated Press).

25 April 1986

The West Berlin *Morgenpost* reports that the documents found at Hasi's flat 'have turned out to be insufficient grounds for keeping Hasi in jail' and 'the evidence against him is getting ever thinner'; Hasi's lawyer presses for his release; unidentified police sources tell Associated Press that there has been 'no progress' on solving the La Belle bombing.

27 April 1986

The *Observer*, drawing on Washington and Bonn sources, reports that the US administration has 'massaged' the intercepts used to prove Libyan complicity in the La Belle bombing in order to make their relevance more clear-cut.

28 April 1986

A West Berlin judge declines to release Ahmed Hasi.

6 May 1986

West Berlin police announce that Hasi and his associate Salameh have confessed to carrying out the 'Friendship Society' bomb attack on 29 March. They do not now think that they were involved in the La Belle attack.

22–23 May 1986

The German newspapers *Die Welt* and *Bild* report an alleged connection between the La Belle bombing and a Libyan shot dead in East Berlin in 2 or 3 May. According to unidentified Intelligence sources Mohammed Ashour, a former Libyan diplomat, was killed on the orders of Colonel Gadaffi because he had passed information on the La Belle bombing to the CIA. US diplomatic sources and the West German government discount the story and West Berlin police spokesman Dieter Piete tells Associated Press that 'there was no ground to suspect Ashour was involved in the discotheque attack'. Associated Press also quote police investigators as saying that there are 'similarities' between the 'Friendship' attack and the La Belle attack (Associated Press, 22 May 1986).

June 1986
(precise date unknown)

Awni Hindawi, cousin of Nezar, arrested in Genoa.

31 July 1986

Volker Kühne for the West Berlin justice department announces that Hasi and Salameh are being charged with the 'Friendship Society' bombing of 29 March. He also says they were trained in Libya in 1985 but carried out the 29 March bombing with Syrian assistance and backing. He says that the investigation into the La Belle bombing should be complete by late summer, that Hasi has denied responsibility and that no one else has been arrested in that case.

24 October 1986

Following the conclusion of the trial of Nezar Hindawi in London, Sir Geoffrey Howe makes a statement in the House of Commons: 'There is no evidence implicating Syria or any other country other than Libya in the bombing of the La Belle discotheque last April.'

17 November 1986

On the first day of the trial of Hasi and Salameh the *Guardian* correspondent reports that 'the La Belle investigations have reached a dead end'.

24 November 1986

Der Spiegel notes that the court has been told of a visit made to Hasi shortly after his arrest on suspicion of the La Belle attack. Two British security agents were introduced to Hasi as Detective Chief Inspector Lloyd and Detective Constable Talbot. Hasi believed one of them to be an Israeli agent. Hasi claimed that he agreed to confess to the 29 March bomb attack and its Syrian backing after being threatened with return to Jordan, where as a militant opponent of King Hussein he would expect to suffer.

	Der Spiegel was told that investigating authorities in London had not heard of the two British agents as named in Court.
26 November 1986	Hasi and Salameh convicted of the 29 March bomb attack.
18 January 1987	The West Berlin *Morgenpost* cites anonymous justice department sources as saying that a letter found on Awni Hindawi (cousin of Nezar, held in Genoa since June 1986) referred both to the La Belle discotheque and a Syrian intelligence agent known as Samer Koukhash (Associated Press, 19 January).

Before letting loose the dogs of war, it is surely an obligation to make sure of the factual evidence on which the decision is made. This Mrs Thatcher failed to do. Yet she continued to brazen it out, claiming that she had evidence that the Libyans were responsible for the La Belle discotheque atrocity.

When the American Sixth Fleet was training its guns on Beirut some months later, the British public must have wondered with Mr D. J. Pugh of Humberside in his letter to the *Guardian*:

Sir—Is the incontrovertible evidence the Americans now say they possess, implicating Syria in the bombing of a Berlin nightclub, the same as the 'incontrovertible' evidence they said they possessed earlier, implicating Libya and Colonel Gadaffi? Or is it different evidence they say they possess?

Nor was there any mention of another reason, which did not surface in public until February 1987 when Seymour Hersh, the well-informed American journalist, suggested in the *New York Times* and in the *Sunday Times* that the primary objective had been to kill Colonel Gadaffi. 'There's no question they were looking for Gadaffi,' said an Air Force Intelligence officer, quoted by Hersh. 'It was briefed that way. They were going to kill him.' Other sources told Hersh that Colonel Gadaffi's family had been sought out because their deaths would lead to a loss of face for him, in that he could not defend his own family. (In the event Colonel Gadaffi's fifteen-month-old adopted daughter was killed, and his wife and eight other children were sent to hospital.)

If the objective was a clandestine attempt to 'take out' Colonel Gadaffi, it would provide a supplementary reason for using F1-11s. On a big ship like a carrier, people talk to one another. Anyone who has been at sea knows that this is inevitable. If there really were a top secret mission to attack the Libyan leader and his family, then there would be a much better chance of preserving secrecy if the instructions were confined to one or two Air Force pilots entrusted with the mission.

Was there a plan to eliminate Colonel Gadaffi and, if so, was Mrs Thatcher told in advance? It may be a long time before the truth emerges, but what is clear is that Mrs Thatcher had plenty of time in which to reflect, and was not forced into the position of giving a snap answer to President Reagan. Her support for his action was unequivocal – whatever lay behind that action.

In 1965, at the height of American euphoria about the war in Vietnam, I was the guest of Bill Carey of the Bureau of the Budget in Washington. I visited Vice President Hubert Humphrey and senators and congressmen in key posts in Lyndon Johnson's Washington. Hearing that a young British Labourite MP was going round Washington, Walter Rostow, then the President's security adviser, operating in the White House basement, sent for me. 'This is *the* nerve centre,' he proudly boasted to me. And so it was.

I relate this story to the fact that there were British Embassy officials present in the basement of the White House on the night of 14/15 April 1986, discussing specific bombing targets with the representatives and advisers of the American President, such as Colonel Oliver North.[1] I am told that the British officials were extremely uneasy at what they were being asked to do. They showed little enthusiasm, and every one of their suggestions was directed towards the reduction of casualties. However, their general instructions from London were all too clear, and if the reduction of casualties appeared in these instructions, it was secondary to the need to go ahead and back Reagan.

So, while detailed negotiations were going on with the Americans in Washington, the House of Commons was being kept in the dark. I knew that Denis Healey had asked for a private notice question, and was astonished that the Shadow Foreign Secretary had not been granted one. This provoked the following exchange on the very afternoon before the Libyan raid:

Mr Tam Dalyell (Linlithgow): On a point of order, Mr Speaker.

Mr Speaker: Does it arise out of questions?

Mr Dalyell: Yes. Precisely because I did not put in a private notice question I feel that, on behalf of several backbenchers, I am entitled to ask whether it is not extraordinary that, in the middle of the crisis concerning Libya and the British bases, the House of Commons is to hear nothing. Would not any visitor consider it extraordinary if we were to spend eight and a half hours debating Sunday trading and yet, as a legislature, be told nothing about the United States or Soviet position or to have a statement on the crisis?

You will know, Mr Speaker, that I have thought for a long time that you are a very superior Speaker to George Thomas. [*Interruption.*]

Mr Speaker: Order. I am enjoying this.

Mr Dalyell: George Thomas made certain judgements of

[1] As reported by Alex Brummer in the *Guardian*.

his own, such as that in April 1982 that the Prime Minister ought to be supported on the south Atlantic issue. We read that in his memoirs. There is no secret about it. That happened during one of the last crises, when he was Speaker, concerning those islands in the south Atlantic. Do you not think, Mr Speaker, that it is matter of some judgement whether circumstances that are a matter of war, or potential war, outside Europe, entitle Parliament to a report from Ministers? There might be a judgement about the safety of British subjects. You know that I am one of those hon. Members who have constituents who are involved, and at risk, near Tripoli. Bearing in mind the circumstances, why does the House not have at least a Foreign Office or Prime Ministerial report on this urgent matter?

In his recent book *The Land That Lost Its Heroes*, Mr Jimmy Burns, correspondent of the *Financial Times* in Buenos Aires from 1981–86, outlined in some detail the arms negotiations between Libya and Argentina which he believes took place during the Falklands War. Mr Burns then concludes: 'The Libyan connection does, moreover, have an important postscript. Gadaffi's involvement in the Falklands War, although tolerated initially by Whitehall, was to colour Mrs Thatcher's relations with Libya following the conflict. Evidence of arms supplies to the Galtieri junta, like the evidence of supplies to the IRA, strained Britain's pragmatism. Although it was never alluded to in public, it must have been at the back of Mrs Thatcher's mind when in April 1986, almost exactly four years after the outbreak of the Falklands War, she fell in four-square behind the unprecedented US bombing of Tripoli.'

I suspect that Mr Burns is right, and that support for Galtieri, plus the murder outside the Libyan Peoples' Bureau of Police Constable Yvonne Fletcher, did a great deal to prepare the ground for Mrs Thatcher's endorsement of President Reagan's plan of attack. At the same time, she might have remembered the 10,000 or so British expatriates working in Libya, and spread throughout that country, working in offices, factories and oil installations. She might also have thought of the 2000 Libyan students studying in British universities and places of higher education, of the 250 aircraft technicians and pilots being trained at Gatwick and Oxford, and of the 7000-strong Libyan community in Britain.

The point is most powerfully put in one of the most moving letters written to *The Times* in recent years:

Other side of Libya story
From Ms J. M. Over

Sir, I am one of thousands of foreign workers in Libya, who naturally deplore terrorism but, even more so, deplore the action of the Americans and the involvement of the British Government in this action.

I am a secretary who lives with other girls and families in apartments above our office block – all British.

I wish to state that the Libyan people have shown us the utmost kindness and concern during the recent air raids. They have left their own families to ensure that we were safe, to the point of staying in the basement of our building with us all night.

The staff in the company restaurant kept working until 11 p.m. at night to ensure that we had a hot meal, constant cups of coffee and ice cream for the four very young children who live in the building. They had started work at 5.30 a.m. and had to return at the same time the following day (all staff were local with families).

The switchboard and telex were manned 24 hours a day to ensure that our anxious relatives could contact us and the militia guards accompanied anyone who wished to move from the basement during the blackout to their apartments on the higher floors. The management had also arranged to take us to their own homes in the case of an emergency.

In another building, which houses only British secretaries, the local residents took them to their own homes to stay with their families so that they were not so frightened and alone.

These are only a few of the many wonderful things these people have done for us. In times of trouble they do not think of themselves and their families; they open their homes to people whose countries have committed these frightening raids on their towns and I thank them from the bottom of my heart for everything they have done. They continually tell us not to worry and that we are thought of as brothers and sisters.

Please print this to show the other side of the story.

Yours faithfully,
JOSEPHINE M. OVER,
Oasis Oil Co. of Libya, Inc.,
Inas Building,
Giaddat Omar El Muktar,
PO Box 395,
Tripoli, Libya,
April 21, 1986.

Before departing from the Prime Minister's behaviour over the Libyan bombing, an examination of her personal style is called for.

There was little or no consultation with political colleagues. For example, that very morning, 14 April, George Younger, MP for Ayr and Defence Secretary of Britain, was interviewed on Radio Ayr. 'Something has got to be done,' said he. 'I think that my colleagues and I are very dubious as to whether a military strike is the best way of doing this. It is liable to hit the wrong people, it creates other tensions in the area. There are a lot of other things that can be done which my colleagues are certainly looking at very hard – further withdrawals of diplomats from offending countries, action like reducing trade and reducing contacts of one sort and another with those who refuse to outlaw terrorism.'

These are hardly the words of a man who expected action to take place that very night. The truth is that the Cabinet Minister most immediately responsible was not consulted, but simply told what he had to do. Does this reflect the workings of a proper Cabinet Government? Michael Heseltine had a point.

Again, what of the other Cabinet Minister most entitled to know: the Foreign Secretary? I asked Sir Geoffrey Howe when he was consulted. Was it before, or was it after, anything could usefully be done on the considered advice of the Foreign Office (which was, as George Younger thought, against the notion of a strike)? On 16 April 1986, Sir Geoffrey told me in the House, 'No evidence emerged during the discussion that any Foreign Minister [of the European Community] was aware during the meeting of a final American decision to attack. For my part, I had no confirmation of any decision by the President, still less of any decision to authorise raids that night, until I came back to London and met the Prime Minister.' The question was properly asked in the Lords by Field Marshal Lord Carver: 'Who was consulted and who agreed?' Officially the Field Marshal has gone unanswered. The truth is that it was Mrs Thatcher alone.

Throughout my political life I have been forcefully struck by the way in which leaders lean over backwards to be different from their predecessors. Harold Wilson was not part of Hugh Gaitskell's Frognal Gardens parties, and therefore had no social relations with his colleagues and Party. Mrs Thatcher will not do things that people think Ted Heath would have done. Equally, President Reagan is highly sensitive to the scorn he heaped on Jimmy Carter for doing so little about the Iranian hostages.

For the real reason, above all, that President Reagan gave his consent, one may turn to his own advisers, as reported on a *World in Action* programme about the bombing in June 1986. In the programme it was admitted that the attack on Libya had less to do with terrorism and more to do with reversing the years of humiliation that had begun with Vietnam. 'You know the United States is brought up on stories that have good guys and bad guys . . . heroes and villains', one adviser said. After the Carter era, Reagan had promised things would be different. But his obvious targets, Syria and Iran, both with records of terrorist action against the United States, have powerful defences and are close to the Soviet Union. So the President turned to Libya, a small country which had often taunted America. Despite the rhetoric, there was no direct link between Gadaffi and events like the hijacking of a TWA jet and the *Achille Lauro*. And three months after the bombing raid there was more concrete evidence that Syria was behind the death of the American serviceman in Berlin, which allegedly provoked it, than that Libya was. Libya was just President Reagan's fall guy in a bizarre display of image- and body-building.

I am no admirer of the President of South Africa, but to my mind Mr Botha was quite justified in making comparisons between what our Prime Minister and President Reagan did together, and the attack, so universally deplored outside South Africa, on Zimbabwe, Zambia and Botswana. And nor is it just the Prime Minister's critics who think along these lines. Ferdinand Mount, writing in the *Spectator* on 24 May 1986, said, 'For the comparison does throw a fascinating if rather eerie light on our confused and contradictory attitudes towards terrorism and the response to terrorism. The two raids are as nearly alike as any two events in an untidy world. The Governments of Zambia, Botswana, and Zimbabwe may not sponsor terrorism in quite the same way as Colonel Gadaffi does; but the distinction is not a crucial one.'

The question must be asked of Downing Street, and of those in the Foreign Office allowed into the 'know' – i.e. those whose loyalty was known to be absolutely for Mrs Thatcher, rather than to the Foreign Secretary: Did they do anything to discourage the United States from taking action against Libya? And if not, why not?

As a postscript to the affair of the bombing of Libya, a not unrelated question ought to be asked. Though there happened to be full involvement of Mrs Thatcher in the use of British bases on this occasion, what would have happened if she had not co-operated? We have already heard from Rear Admiral Carroll that the plan was prepared on a use-the-bases-first-ask-questions-afterwards eventuality, and I suspect the Americans would have gone blithely ahead.

On 17 April 1986 I was sitting in front of James Callaghan when he told the House of Commons that, from his long experience as Father of the House and ex-Prime Minister, 'it never occurred to anyone' when US bombers arrived in the UK in 1950 that these aircraft would be used for non-NATO purposes.

Nor did it for three decades. But on 7 March 1983, there appeared in *The Times* from Gene La Rocque, Director of the Center for Defense Information to which Rear Admiral Carroll also belongs, a lead letter. What Admiral La Rocque said was this:

I cannot see how the interests of the NATO nations can be well served by comforting deceptions about who controls nuclear weapons. I favor close cooperation within NATO and an effective defense for all NATO members. But we must face facts. American nuclear weapons are American nuclear weapons, whether they are located in the United States, at sea, or in Europe.

The American nuclear weapons in Europe, and those that are to come, are totally under the control of the US Government. They will be used only if and when the US Government decides to do so. No prior understandings or arrangements about consultation will alter this fact. No member of NATO has a veto power over American nuclear weapons.

In a crunch situation, what use is the distinction between nuclear and non-nuclear weapons? The awkward truth is that the President of the United States, as Commander in Chief of the US Armed Forces, is constitutionally forbidden to accept any veto or restriction by a foreign power, anywhere in the world, on the use of American forces, if he is advised by his joint chiefs of staff that the security of the United States is threatened. This is not something that can be set aside by any President, no matter how good his personal relations may appear to be with another head of state. This is also why successive Administrations in Washington have never accepted a copy of the British version of the 'agreement' between America and Britain on bases. Just before he died, Dean Acheson spoke admiringly of Attlee's attempt to achieve the promise of consultation, but added, 'we had to unachieve that'. And thus it has remained. British Ministers of both political parties have always postulated convenient war scenarios where international tension rises slowly, so that NATO's supposedly well-oiled machinery will allow time for views to be passed back and forth across the Atlantic. But as in the case of the invasion of Grenada, things often happen so quickly that there is no time to consult. Perhaps, after British failure to consult over the Falklands and the *Belgrano*, there is no disposition to consult. Gerry Northam, in his *Listener* article of 15 May 1986, put the position most succinctly: 'it may be impolitic to say so, but the fact of the 1952 "joint decision" agreement is that the United States President would make the decision, and the British Prime Minister would make it a joint decision.'

4

Breaking Coal

It is not only in international-related affairs, but also on Mrs Thatcher's domestic front that the question of her deceitful conduct has raised its head. The 1984 miners' strike was not about wages, but pit closures. On account of the industrial recession, the demand for coal was significantly lower than forecast. Over-production had led to falling prices. While other European nations were helping their coal industries to weather the storm, Mrs Thatcher's Government chose that of all moments to insist on a viable coal industry in Britain.

Harold Macmillan was fond of an adage. In British politics, said the veteran of Flanders, 'we do not take on the Brigade of Guards, the Roman Catholic Church, or the National Union of Mineworkers'. The point he was making was that these were highly cohesive groups who would stand together against all-comers if roused. There was something special about them.

For my own part, I have always believed that there is indeed something special about miners. Ever since my father arranged for me to go on a visit down a coal mine as a fourteen-year-old boy, I have had nothing but respect for those who win coal for the rest of us. And before people start criticising miners, justifiably or unjustifiably, my gut reaction is to enquire, 'When were you last down a pit?'. Unless at some time in one's life one has crawled along a difficult seam during the actual operation of winning coal, I doubt if one is entitled to an opinion, worthy of respect, about coal miners.

When, in 1962, I became a candidate in the selection conference procedure to stand at a by-election in West Lothian, it was with the support and nomination of the National Union of Shale-oil Miners. It was one of their last acts as a Union when their last General Secretary, the late Joe Heaney, nominated me. Rather shallower than coal mines, shale mines were even more dangerous, through gas and damp and the brittle nature of the shale which could cause severe injury. Now the pink bings, the shale heaps, of the Lothians are the only remaining testimony to what was once a thriving industry, producing high-grade aero-engine fuel and industrial wax.

At the selection conference, attended by 162 delegates from constituency Labour parties and affiliated trade unions, I was also given the nomination of the branch of the National Association of Colliery Oversmen, Deputies and Shot Firers (NACODS), Kinneil Branch (Kinneil was the huge Bo'ness colliery). The reason for this was personal rather than political. I had been a teacher at Bo'ness Academy, and had taken school football teams to win the Final of the Scottish Schoolboys' Cup, and subsequently abroad to Spain, Portugal and Gibraltar, the Palatinate, Sweden, Denmark and Russia. The grandfather of one of the boys, an elderly miner who had the nomination in his gift, liked the way I treated his difficult grandson, who was a footballer, and thought that he would reward me with the NACODS nomination.

Then the late and unforgettable Abe Moffat, Communist President of the Scottish Miners, heard what had happened and blew his considerable top. He wanted the seat for a sixty-three-year-old colleague whom he wished to get out of his own office. Many people in the Scottish Left laughed and said, 'But Abe, Tam Dalyell was nominated by a constituent branch of *your* own trade union.' Abe and his brother, Alec, were unprintable at the time. Ribaldry is a great force in politics. Delegates and their organisations who would not have given me, a twenty-nine-year-old, another look, thought that I must be a person of considerable substance to have upset the dreaded Abe so much – and gave me their vote. (A great many more delegates knew me personally and wanted a local man, given the Scottish Nationalist climate and the fact that my predecessor had lived in the South and visited West Lothian less and less.)

I was selected on the fourth ballot on a Sunday afternoon in May 1962. From the moment the result of the ballot was announced, no candidate nor MP could have had greater kindness or more help from the mining community in Scotland, and the officials of the National Union of Mineworkers. When I think what they were being asked to swallow, in the shape of an Old Etonian, with many views which they did not share, I cannot speak warmly enough of the generosity of a generation that is now largely departed.

In the summer of 1962, during the Parliamentary recess, I spent a day going down to the coal faces at Woodend, Polkemmet, Whitrigg, Riddochhill, Easton and Kinneil. Through my constituents the late Willie Collins (who had me crawling the full length of the most difficult seam of the old-fashioned anthracite Woodend pit) and Willie McLean, Secretary of the Scottish Miners – prominent British Communists both – I came to have a good relationship with Michael McGahey, a man of great charm, wit and intelligence, and other miners' leaders. Lawrence Daly, General Secretary of the National Union of Mineworkers and one of the greatest trade union orators of the 1960s, was my friend and constituent.

Paradoxically, about the coal industry itself I have very ambiguous feelings. I, along with many miners, would not like a son of mine to spend thirty years working in the bowels of the earth. One of the duties which really moved me as a young MP was visiting erstwhile miners in their homes to try to help sort out their compensation cases. I remember a score of men, once tough and strong, unable to mount their own staircase for want of breath. The price of coal was pneumoconiosis, and too often life itself. If people romanticise the coal industry, I just recollect attending too many funerals of young and middle-aged miners, killed in pit accidents or withering away through dust in the lung, to entertain those kinds of hallucinations.

Many excellent MPs represent, equally excellently, areas with which they have had little to do before they became MPs, and with which they have little contact after they retire or are defeated. If, like me and others, you are a local man or woman, brought up in the area, and expecting to spend the rest of your days in the area, relationships are somewhat naturally a little different. Those of us, not necessarily miners, who lived in the coalfields had rather special emotions about the miners' strike which began in March 1984. It was polarisation, and potential mayhem, in *our* community, *our* home area. Like many Labour MPs in other areas, I used regularly for months, getting up at 4.30 a.m. on a Monday morning, to go to the picket line at Polkemmet[1] as a calming (if often marginal) influence. Like many others, I gave a good deal of money to the miners, saw what their families were going through, and was consumed with suppressed anger at what was happening to my country. So the miners' strike was, and always will be, a very personal event in my life. There was an emotional and personal background.

Equally, for Mrs Thatcher, there was a personal and emotional background – albeit of a very different kind. Suffice to say that she was a member of Edward Heath's Cabinet, which had been brought down by the circumstances surrounding the miners' strike of 1974, and the three-day week. Above all else, it mattered in life to Mrs Margaret Hilda Thatcher that she should be seen to be different from Ted Heath.

The conclusion which Mrs Thatcher learned from 1974,

[1] At the request of both the local officials and members of the National Union of Mineworkers, and of the Lothians and Borders Police.

and indeed from the 1972 humiliation at the hands of the miners, was that a Government should not be seen to involve itself in a wage-fixing, even in the public sector.

Although, as we shall see, Mrs Thatcher as Prime Minister did become involved in the 1984–85 strike, the Government could persuasively claim that it was an onlooker for much of the time. Certainly Ministers and their officials were never physically present in the negotiations, and this turned out to be a great advantage for Mrs Thatcher, and simultaneously a great disadvantage for an NUM leadership which was trying to focus the blame on the Prime Minister.

On 10 May 1984, I was sitting next to Jack Dormand, chairman of the Parliamentary Labour Party and MP for Easington, County Durham, when he asked this question of the Prime Minister:

> **Mr Dormand:** 'Will the Prime Minister confirm that a line in a well-known prayer, which she recited to the nation in 1979, "grant that I may seek . . . to understand rather than to be understood", still guides her in her duties? If so, will she now intervene in the miners' dispute as the only possible way of breaking the deadlock? Will she cease to play the role of Pontius Pilate by washing her hands of the dispute? Is that not the way to seek greater understanding?'

This was the answer he got:

> **The Prime Minister:** 'I seek both to understand and to be understood. I hope that I do not have great difficulty in either. I believe that the way to end the coal dispute is by taking advantage of the consultation procedures which exist and which are being attended by some of the miners' unions.'

The truth is that it was *not* left to the consultation procedures. At crucial moments in the dispute, while claiming everything was up to Hobart House,[1] Mrs Thatcher was not only up to her neck in the dispute, but actually preventing the men involved in those very consultation procedures from reaching a settlement. Whatever suspicions many of us might have entertained at the time, we could not prove Mrs Thatcher's complicity. The proof has only recently come to light.

I must confess that although I had read a number of his articles in *The Times*, I had little real conception of the role played by Mr David Hart in the miners' strike until the autumn of 1986. Then, in a favourable review of Martin Adeney and John Lloyd's book, *Loss without Limit: The Miners' Strike 1984–85*, Mr Ross McKibbin wrote: 'There is much inside information and a number of curious individuals come to light, among them David Hart, a libertarian millionaire who saw the dispute in apocalyptic terms, played an important part in organising and (apparently) financing the working miners' litigation, exercised a strong ideological influence on Mr MacGregor, and astonishingly 'issued orders in MacGregor's name' when the NCB Chairman was abroad.'[2]

For an investigative politician, the importance of book reviews cannot be over-estimated. The trouble is that most MPs do not find time to read books, and are much the poorer for it. What I did already know was that in August 1984 Sir Hector Laing, Chairman of United Biscuits, had begun a public fund for the working miners and for their lawyers' fees. I saw a copy of his appeal circulated among business leaders, under the by-line of a quotation from Edmund Burke: 'All that is needed for evil to triumph is that good men do nothing.' Now, United Biscuits gave £43,000 to Conservative Party funds for the 1983 general election, and if Sir Hector was appealing for help for Ken Foulstone and Bob Taylor, the two Yorkshire miners who had had the strike declared illegal in the High Court, it

[1] Headquarters of the National Coal Board.
[2] From *London Review of Books*, 23 October 1986.

could only be with the acquiescence, if not approval, of the Prime Minister. He is, after all, one of her closest advisers. Another Prime Ministerial in-grouper, Lord Hanson, gave £80,000 to Conservative Party funds in 1983 and substantial support to the working miners. It stretches the imagination too far to suppose that Lord Hanson did not check out what he was doing with Downing Street. Sarah Hogg, daughter of John Boyd-Carpenter, then chairman of the Carlton Club, and wife of Douglas Hogg, MP for Grantham (about to be promoted to a Junior Minister's position at the Home Office), was acting as a public relations adviser to the National Working Miners' Committee. This did not happen without the Prime Ministerial okay, either.

My curiosity aroused by Ross McKibbin, I turned to Adeney and Lloyd's text. The trouble about so much of what has been written about the miners' strike is that it comes from a partisan quarter. However, *Loss without Limit* is a bit different. Martin Adeney is the Industrial Editor of BBC TV News, and was previously Industrial Correspondent of the *Sunday Telegraph*, and Labour Correspondent for the *Guardian*, with specialist knowledge of the coal industry. Lloyd was Industrial Editor of the *Financial Times* before becoming Editor of the *New Statesman*. They are seasoned, careful and discriminating authors.

The considered judgement of Adeney and Lloyd is that the use of the law against the National Union of Mineworkers by its members was not pre-ordained. And from my personal experience, the move came as an almighty shock to miners on the picket line in Scotland. It was, we now learn, the result of deliberate calculation in which two men, both millionaire farmers, played important parts.

The first was Peter Walker, Secretary of State for Energy. Walker's part was to make sure that the Government was not seen to be deploying what could be broadly termed 'Tory laws' against the mining community. In my judgement, had the imposition of 'Tory laws' on the miners been the Government's only resource, it would have failed in its intentions. But no one will ever know for certain.

What is certain is that the haemorrhage of will to maintain solidarity of the strike started inside the NUM, when some miners themselves began to use the courts against the union in relation to picketing. But it is clear to me from various sources that the idea of using the courts against their own fellow miners did not simply happen by a process akin to spontaneous combustion among rank-and-file miners. The tactic originated in the rich and relatively well paid Nottinghamshire coalfield, with its highish wages and the legacy of Spencerism.[1]

And this is where the second man, David Hart, a property developer and a farmer with a consuming passion for politics, comes in. Over a three-month period, David Hart travelled 35,000 miles to put together a network of cells of disaffected miners, ready to organise a return to work. Out of this activity grew the Union of Democratic Mine-workers.

In his own book about the strike, *The Enemies Within*, Ian MacGregor described Hart in crusading terms:

David is a curious character. He is forty-two years old; an old Etonian who had made and lost a fortune in the 1970s property boom. He is a novelist and a writer of occasional articles for *The Times*. He could, and did, circulate just as easily among the miners of Nottingham-shire as he did in the highest political circles. When I first met him at an Institute of Economic Affairs lunch on 2 July 1984 he had already spent a considerable amount of time in Nottingham, reporting for *The Times*, with a mounting sense of frustration and anger at what was happening to the men who wanted to work. I had worked with his brother, Tim, at Lehman Bros in New York and, as we chatted, I began to realise that he was the man I had been looking for.

[1] In 1926 the Nottinghamshire miners continued to work, abetted by Spencer who was a Nottinghamshire MP.

On 2 May 1984, David Hart put his basic view in *The Times*: 'Such extraparliamentary opposition cannot be defeated in the body politic by high coal stocks at the power stations or by the police upholding the law. These men will have to be defeated in the soul politic, too.' This reveals a minimum of understanding about the concern for jobs in the kind of area I live in and represent. What it does reveal is a deep affinity to the concept of the 'enemies within' – the insulting reference to the miners of this country used by Mrs Thatcher.

Hart's strategy was to encourage case after case taken to the courts by the working miners. This bogged down the NUM leadership in endless, time-consuming legal wrangles, on a pitch where they were playing away from home. Most miners' officials had little idea of the law, other than in compensation matters, and often retreated (to my personal knowledge) into exhausted bewilderment. Hart on the other hand knew what he was doing, and succeeded in doing it. His was also a direct assault on the NUM's precious funds.

Adeney and Lloyd's version of Hart's role is this: 'The centre of these actions was, of course, Nottinghamshire, and here the figure of David Hart assumed a central role. It is true to say that the working miners' legal actions proceeded from their own initiatives: but it is also the case that Hart shaped their initially uncertain moves, linked them to powerful sources of financial and other support, and helped them feel that they were part of a crusade.'

I go further than the authors. Talking to people involved, and visiting Mansfield in a political capacity, I am quite clear that before Hart arrived in Nottinghamshire, the notion of actually dragging the NUM through the courts was no more than pub talk among the most dissatisfied union members. Without Hart, any such talk would have evaporated. In every real sense the initial moves were Hart's. He not only shaped the moves of others, he was the catalyst. And crucially he was the conduit for the cash.

The money was almost certainly not from his own

pocket. His father was one of the founders of the merchant bank, Henry Ansbacher, involved in the secondary banking crash of 1974 – for which Hart is said never to have forgiven Ted Heath. David Hart was discharged from bankruptcy in 1978, and began to run a property business from an office in Brook Street, London. But it was not his links with Ansbacher or any other bank that produced most money for Hart's cause in 1984. It was because he had the imprimatur of the Prime Minister for what he was up to. Hart was the centre of the spider's web of the working miners, putting out feelers to Scotland, Durham and other coalfields. But the spider mistress herself was the Prime Minister. Seeing himself as a knight in shining armour, as some kind of St George defending Freedom against the dragon of Tyranny, Hart was a heaven-sent tool.[1]

Hart developed a weird hold over MacGregor. Initially MacGregor ignored the working miners, regarding them as simply peripheral. Some months later, MacGregor had come to see the working miners as freedom fighters, heroes in the struggle for British democracy itself. This was directly due to Hart's influence. Such was his hold over the Coal Board chairman that, to the consternation of other senior people in Hobart House, by the last days of the strike Hart could be found in the chairman's office as often as Ian MacGregor himself. In the autumn of 1984, when MacGregor was temporarily in the United States, Hart actually issued orders in MacGregor's name.

It was David Hart also who masterminded a coup which I witnessed at first hand. On the Friday before delegates started gathering for the Labour Party conference at Blackpool, and while the NEC of the Party was deliberating, Mr Justice Nicholls granted an injunction restraining the National Union of Mineworkers or its Yorkshire area from

[1] It should also be said that I have knowledge that in arguments about the Strategic Defence Initiative, about policing and educational policy, to name but a few topics, Hart has had access to the Prime Minister, without the filter of the relevant Secretary of State.

seeking to persuade its members not to cross the picket lines. The NUM and its officials were to be restrained from 'describing or treating the strike or any picket line in the said Yorkshire areas as "official" or words to the like effect'. Unwisely, in my view, Arthur Scargill went on Channel Four News to declaim that whatever the courts said, the strike in Yorkshire and everywhere else was official: 'and I'm going to say this, quite clearly: that any miner in this union who urges or crosses a picket line in defiance of our union's instructions runs the risk of being disciplined under the rules . . . There is no High Court judge going to take away the democratic right of our union to deal with internal affairs. We are an independent democratic trade union.'

Payne and Fearn, the lawyers in Nottinghamshire with whom Hart was in cahoots, had their video running as Scargill spoke. The following day, while the Labour Party conference delegates were going through their compositing procedures for motions, the lawyers were busy preparing affidavits, and they applied to the High Court for leave to give notice of contempt proceedings as soon as they could. The orders were issued early on Monday morning, but the lawyers were on the spot. They had to have them served on Arthur Scargill that very day, the Monday, or their validity would expire. They could not get to Blackpool in time to do so. But David Hart had it organised. He had a chartered helicopter on call, which came to his mansion, Coldham Hall, near Bury in Lancashire. He flew in it to London Heliport, collected the process server who had been lined up, and put him down at Blackpool Airport, together with a *Daily Express* photographer whom he had lined up. They sneaked into the Labour Party Conference with a borrowed press pass (a gross abuse), and I saw the notice of motion and legal documentation being served on an astonished Arthur Scargill, to the sheer fury of delegates at the Party conference. What would Mrs Thatcher have said about the activities of anyone, after the Brighton bombing, who got into the Conservative Party conference under false pretences? Yet David Hart was doing her general bidding.

It was David Hart who prompted Mr Colin Clarke and fifteen other members of the Working Miners' Committee, after difficulty in the sequestration of funds, to go back to court to call for the twenty-five members of the National Executive of the NUM to be made personally liable for the £200,000 fine, and for the NUM trustees, Messrs Scargill, Heathfield and McGahey, to be replaced by a receiver appointed by the court.

It was also David Hart who brought Tim Bell, a central figure in the Saatchi and Saatchi advertising agency in its successful promotion of Mrs Thatcher in the 1979 election, into Hobart House. Bell and Hart clashed with Ned Smith, the long-serving and caring personnel director, over the decision in June 1984 to send a letter under Ian Mac-Gregor's name to all miners.

According to Ned Smith, an interview with Ian Mac-Gregor in *The Times* of 12 June 1984, in the middle of negotiations which Smith believed were going well, wholly destroyed them. MacGregor expressed himself in his usual blunt way and any atmosphere of conciliation was shattered. This interview had been set up by David Hart,[1] with Downing Street's knowledge, and the effect was exactly as Hart and Thatcher – though not MacGregor – intended.

On 22 August 1984 Channel Four arranged a live TV debate between an NCB representative and Arthur Scargill. Ned Smith was to have put the Coal Board case. In the afternoon at about 5 p.m., MacGregor decided to cancel the programme. Smith stormed home, furious, whereupon MacGregor did the programme himself. This again was Hart's idea, and Hart acted as the chairman's minder. (During the argument MacGregor denied the existence of any peace initiative by my friend and col-

---

[1] I know for a fact that Hart was responsible for the interview from a source who was present when he expressed himself pleased at having done it.

league, the Labour Energy spokesman, Stan Orme – a denial he later had to withdraw, in an abject excuse about misunderstandings.)

On 13 September 1984, *The Times* published an article by David Hart entitled 'Seeds of a Union revolution'. It praised the National Working Miners' Committee and revealed that at least a dozen new court actions against the NUM were planned. 'All actions that have been started so far have been successful,' he claimed.

Then, the following day, *The Times* carried the text of a proposed settlement with a pejorative commentary, at a time when Smith and his colleagues thought that they were within 'an inch of a settlement'. This wrecked the negotiations once more. I now know that this was fixed by David Hart in conjunction with the late Charles Douglas Home, then editor of *The Times*, whose role, *de mortuis nil nisi bonum*, was malign. (I say this with sorrow since he had been a personal friend of mine for twenty years.)

The whole style of Hart's operation was that of a thug. For example, Michael Eaton, the NCB North Yorkshire director, was summoned down to London by the Deputy Chairman James Cowan, but he was met by David Hart who took him to his Bond Street office and talked of 'screwing Scargill'.

By October 1984, Hart had become the greatest influence on MacGregor. In a memorandum written for the Chairman on 10 October, Hart made it clear that the strike was political, and that its outcome was no longer the exclusive concern of the management of the NCB – if indeed it ever had been. If the narrow interest of the NCB clashed with the 'wider public interest', it must be the public interest which took precedence. It was, opined Hart, *not* in the public interest or the national interest for a settlement to be reached, because any agreement would be seen as a surrender to Scargill. Hart, this millionaire farmer, had the cheek to advise MacGregor that what was needed were better public relations, an end to all negotiations, withdrawal of the commitment to no compulsory redundancies after November 1984, the sacking of all miners convicted of offences, and the closure of pits in danger. Hart inveigled MacGregor into using some of his own slogans such as 'individual liberty' and 'the war against tyranny', and ill-disguised political sentiments.

Even Peter Walker became uneasy to his friends about Hart's involvement, though what may have touched an even rawer nerve with the Energy Secretary was what he learned about Hart's close relationship with the Prime Minister. I have been told of a hostile and acid telephone call when Walker is reported as saying that he did not think it prudent for the strike to be seen to be run from Claridge's, where Hart stayed.

As in the Falklands, what mattered for the Prime Minister was victory for its own sake – regardless of whether there was a long-term solution to be had, regardless of the long-term bitterness between members of the same communities, the same villages in Britain. 'What did your family do in '84?' will be a question that will be asked for a long time in the coalfields.

Walker and others of a similar healing view were the object of a scarcely veiled attack in *The Times* of 17 November 1984 by David Hart:

Although most members of the Cabinet are reported to be absolutely sound at least on this issue, from time to time certain senior ministers have arranged for inspired articles to appear in newspapers pointing out that many members of the Government, mindful of the cost to the country of the strike, mindful of the cost in suffering to the communities, are most anxious for a settlement. One minister recently declared on television, at a sensitive moment during the negotiations, that there could be no winners and no losers in the dispute, a very typical Will to Lose remark.

Hart first met Mrs Thatcher at the dinner for policy studies in 1980, and has frequently claimed that he 'has access to the Prime Minister'. I learn, from a senior Cabinet Minister, that these claims are certainly substantiated.

Two years after the miners' strike, on Philip Whitehead's programme on Channel Four on 17 July 1986, David Hart truculently told viewers that in the summer and autumn of 1984, he had given advice to the Prime Minister that 'it was politically undesirable to settle'. Precisely. And, alas, the advice was taken.

But then the miners' strike for Mrs Thatcher was not about the national interest. It was about domestic politics. Mrs Thatcher revealed volumes about her own attitude of mind when she saw fit to draw a comparison between the Argentines during the Falklands War as 'the enemy without' and the National Union of Mineworkers as 'the enemy within'. The strike was not just another case of Mrs Thatcher winning a fight at all costs. It was a case of her setting up one more opportunity of *being seen* to win, in order to strengthen her public image. The miners' strike cost this country £3.75 billion.[1] That was the price paid to satisfy the Prime Minister's appetite for looking good in the ratings.

[1] Supplementary Note by HM Treasury to House of Commons and Civil Service Treasury Committee, Appendix 7 to 2nd Report in 1985–86 session, House of Commons Paper 57.

5

Making a Secret Society

'Having thoroughly searched the offices of a dissident magazine, the secret police then worked through the night removing documents from the headquarters of the broadcasting organisation.'

This was the quotation in italics at the head of the leading article on Monday 2 February 1987 in the *Glasgow Herald*, established in 1783 and not given to alarmist views. The opening paragraph of this Conservative newspaper's leader then went on:

'It is not of Eastern Europe that we write but our own dear free country. The actions of the Government in the Zircon affair began by seeming merely incompetent. They now appear incomprehensible, and worse, sinister.'

On Saturday 31 January, having finished my morning MP's surgeries in Fauldhouse and Stoneyburn, villages in the south of West Lothian, I was driving towards Broxburn, now in the constituency of my friend and Parliamentary neighbour, Robin Cook, to meet shop stewards about the closure of the Golden Wonder crisp factory. I switched on the one o'clock news on the car radio. The first headline was that apparently the police were in the BBC's Queen Margaret Drive building in Glasgow – a most familiar building to any Scots MP. My gut reaction was to turn my car round, get onto the M8 at Whitburn, and head for Glasgow to see what I could do. But there was a redundancy meeting, and people's jobs were at stake. So I did the next best thing, which was to stop my car at the Blackburn, West Lothian supermarket, find a telephone box that had not been vandalised, and get through to the ever-vigilant Chris Moncrieff of the Press Association to voice protest.

But the events in the middle of the day on Saturday 31 January were as nothing to what I heard on the 7 a.m. news the following morning, Sunday 1 February. Police, in force, were lugging loads of documents out of the second biggest offices of the BBC in Britain. Dispensing with my accustomed porridge, I was on my way to my car when my wife – rightly, I think, in the event – cautioned me about getting mixed up with the police on the grounds that I could get caught in an argument with them about impeding officers carrying out their job. Kathleen and I were also, both of us, sensitive to my being involved in what might be seen as a gimmick, which would irritate my Parliamentary colleagues. And the physical presence of a controversial Labour MP might not do the BBC's case much good.

I did not realise at that point how compliant the BBC leadership, under the direction of assistant Director General Alan Protheroe, had turned out to be. Left to themselves, I have little doubt that the working journalists of BBC Scotland would have displayed more spunk. In a number of other countries, the reaction would have been less muted. By chance, Howard Simons, managing editor of the *Washington Post* during the Watergate affair, happened to be in London at the time. He expressed himself astonished and appalled by the attacks on the British media. He drawled to Donald Trelford, editor of the *Observer*[1], 'If the police had gone into the *Post*, they would have found Kay Graham lying in the doorway to stop them.' Alas, there was no one around in Glasgow to match the legendary and formidable Mrs Graham, owner of the *Washington Post*. 'Where,' asks Trelford, 'were our society's self-proclaimed defenders of Truth, Freedom,

[1] *Observer*, 8 February 1987.

and Democracy? Not lying across doorways to protect the media, that's for sure.'

What was all the fuss about? For an answer to this question, far-fetched though it may seem at first, the reader will have to be patient and wait until later in the chapter. What it was *not* about, for sure, was the technology of geostationary satellites.

Let us chronicle events. On Sunday 18 January 1987, the *Observer* front page carried an 'exclusive': 'BBC gag on £500 million defence secret' under the by-line of their media editor, Richard Brooks. As I and others read it, the priority point of the article was not the nature of the project aired in the programme which the then Director General Alasdair Milne had banned, but the different issue that half a billion pounds had been kept from the scrutiny of Parliament, through the Public Accounts Committee. Having served in the 1960s on the PAC under three Chairmen, I am alert to anyone who attempts to mess around with the PAC. It is not only the oldest, but by far the best serviced (through the Comptroller and Auditor General's Office) of all Commons Committees. The reason why I jumped to the conclusion that any ban by the BBC on one of its own programmes could have little to do with the real interests of security was that the go-ahead had been given, we were told, by Alan Protheroe, himself a member of the D-Notice Committee. My scepticism was enhanced when I was told that two men known to me personally, and both heavyweights – Sir Frank Cooper, ex-Permanent Secretary, and Professor Sir Ronald Mason, Chief Scientist of the Ministry of Defence throughout the Falklands War – had participated.

When it emerged that the source of the commotion was some geostationary satellite that we were proposing to hoist up over the Indian Ocean, scepticism spawned more scepticism. Geostationary satellites are not nowadays really very special creatures. From my *New Scientist* background, Skynet IV, if not the actual code-name Zircon, was within my corpus of background knowledge. After all,

I had on my shelf James Bamford's *The Puzzle Palace*, going into some 400 pages of detail about America's National Security Agency, and its special relationship with Britain's GCHQ. I had also looked at Jeffrey Richelson and Desmond Ball's *The Ties that Bind*, about intelligence co-operation between Britain, America, Canada, Australia and New Zealand, which goes into depth about signals intelligence. Subsequently, I was reminded of the *Interspace* newsletter of February 1985, when its editor Roger Stanyard produced technical details of the elevation of Skynet IV, and information about the work being done by British Aerospace and Marconi.

The subscribers to this periodical include most of the high-tech companies, GCHQ, and for certain the relevant technological institute, Intersputnik, in Moscow. Without exaggeration, the Soviets were receiving the supposedly hyper-sensitive information through their letter-box. In any case, as soon as a satellite appeared over the Indian Ocean, it would be picked up by Soviet satellites. Well might Sir Frank Cooper on the very programme suggest that everyone would know of its existence, 'including schoolchildren in Milton Keynes'.

As usual, the trouble is, from my personal viewing of the programme, that it creates political embarrassment – that, on costs, there has been a flagrant breach of promise to Parliament. There was an attempt at a justification by Cooper that it would relieve us of relying on America (and preserve the illusion that Britain is a great power) – but that assumed that somehow Britain could take on the Soviet Union alone, without the involvement of the USA. Then it transpired from Sir Frank that a satellite might be good for 'macro-reasons'. Was this supposed to mean a seat for Britain at some top table? Well, Mrs Thatcher was not invited to Reykjavik. Admittedly, industrial intelligence-gathering is a growth area, and unless you put your money on the table, the Americans are sure you will not get anything from their trough. But all such considerations are a far cry from security.

What happened in the small hours of Sunday morning, 1 February 1987, was a polite gathering of police, lawyers and BBC executives in the Controller's office in Queen Margaret Drive. As I shall argue, the police purpose was not fundamentally or technically a lawful one. Although their ostensible objective was to find evidence about the banned 'Zircon' programme, made by the BBC in Scotland, it was clear even at that early stage that their instructions were to teach the corporation a lesson.

Picture the scene. For more than eighteen hours, the police had literally been in occupation of the newly renovated Broadcasting House. Then Detective Chief Inspector Stewart of Strathclyde Police made it clear that they had grown tired of waiting for the BBC to make up its mind to comply with the search warrant. Egged on by the senior Metropolitan Police officer present, Mr Williams, who was in reality calling the tune,[1] Inspector Stewart said that he wanted compliance and wanted it quickly. I am assured that his actual words were, 'You can do it the easy way, or the hard way.'

The 'easy' way was to get hold of the film editors and library staff to empty all the film material of the Duncan Campbell–Brian Barr *Secret Society* series into waiting police vans before dawn. The alternative option – the 'hard way' – was that the whole huge building would be overrun by police and taken apart in the search for evidence. I am told on first-hand authority that Inspector Stewart said threateningly, 'My patience is running out.' He gave the BBC executives just ten minutes to select the 'easy' way, and start extracting their staff from their Sunday morning beds – if 3.15 a.m. be considered the Sabbath morning.

Alan Protheroe capitulated.

The police had appeared undeterred by the fact that in the middle of the night in Edinburgh Lord Clyde, a senior

---

[1] I was told this by a senior member of Strathclyde police committee.

judge of the Court of Session (the Scottish High Court),
had ruled that the original search warrant was unlawful.
Actually, I know now that the Scottish police, or at least
some of their senior officers, had proverbial kittens when
they were informed of the substance of Lord Clyde's ruling.
They have daily relations with the High Court, and the
last thing their training suggested to them was that they
should become entangled with the judges of the Scottish
Court. But then, the Met. was in charge, the whole operation was, as we shall see, run from London and not from
Scotland, and those in real charge could not care a fig.
Reassured that this was not really their business, the
Scottish police went to get new warrants.

Nor was it a matter of much concern to them that the
BBC's solicitors pointed out on their return, as persistently
as lawyers could, that all they had done was change two
words in an unlawful warrant. Coolly, where the highest
court in Scotland had made it clear that their warrant was
too wide, the police had returned with a warrant which they
intended to interpret even more widely. The explanation of
this *prima facie* extraordinary and uncharacteristic behaviour by the Scottish police is that they had sought and been
given assurances by their Metropolitan Police visitors.

I believe the sources who told me that the Strathclyde
Police were queasy and reluctant when they were asked to
go into the BBC. This was understandable. Scotland is a
smaller place than England, and our relationships tend to
be rather personal. Strathclyde Police have day-to-day
working relations with the Scottish media, not least BBC
Scotland. They were being asked by London to foul their
own nest.

Even the date on the warrant was altered from 30
January (a Friday) to Saturday 31 January. And the paramount consideration in this was not pursuit of justice,
but avoidance of political embarrassment caused by the
presence in the building on that Friday of Malcolm Rifkind
MP, Secretary of State for Scotland, and Donald Dewar
MP for a *Question Time* programme. Besides, it is always

useful to remember that if you are going to do anything controversial in Britain, it is best, as with the Falklands War, started at the weekend, when a lot of people are in the countryside.

Naturally, the Strathclyde Police quizzed the Metropolitan Police as to exactly where their authority came from. I am told that the first answer they were given mentioned the name of Bernard Sheldon – Bernard Sheldon being the legal adviser to the Security Services whose advice was sought and given as to whether to prosecute Mr Peter Wright (when advice on the same subject from the responsible Law Officer, Sir Michael Havers, was neither sought nor given).

Then, hours later, after Lord Clyde's pronouncement from the High Court in Edinburgh, the Scottish police, being decent, concerned professional police officers, pressed again as to the authority on which they were being asked to act. By this time, they had a fairly shrewd idea of the national outcry which was bound to ensue, and of their own position at the sharp end of the action.

'It has been discussed at the highest level,' they were told by the Met. 'And what is "the highest level"?' one senior police officer enquired. 'It is being done on the authority of Downing Street,' he was told.[1] Note that I do not claim that the police were told that it was done on the authority of the Prime Minister, or on the authority of Mrs Thatcher. The expression that I believe to have been used was the 'authority of Downing Street'.

In the February darkness of a Glasgow Sabbath morning, the rule of law had become immaterial. It now transpires that not only were legal corners cut, but that what was done was downright illegal.

Under Section 9 of the Official Secrets Act of 1911 a search warrant can be granted if there is reasonable ground for suspecting that an offence under the Act has been

---

[1] I am afraid readers will have to take this serious allegation on trust, as being from unnamed Scottish sources.

committed, or is about to be committed. According to the terms of the Act the person who can grant the search warrant and who must be satisfied that there are reasonable grounds for suspicion is a Justice of the Peace.

The legal justification for the police raid on the BBC's Scottish headquarters in Glasgow and for the seizure of various films, tapes and documents was a warrant granted under section 9 of the 1911 Act. But that warrant was not granted by a Justice of the Peace. It was granted by a sheriff.

If the reader will bear with me, it is important to go into some detail here. A number of Acts of Parliament which confer powers or duties on Scottish Justices of the Peace go on to provide expressly that for the purposes of that particular Act, 'justice' shall be read as including 'sheriff'. The Official Secrets Act contains *no such provision*.

A search warrant granted by someone who has no legal power or authority to grant it is valueless, and any search of premises or seizure of property carried out under it would be unlawful.

If the Official Secrets Act does not define JP in such a way as to include a sheriff, is there any other method whereby a sheriff could acquire power to grant a warrant under the Act? He would obviously have that power if, whenever someone was appointed to be a sheriff, he was also as a matter of course made a JP. But that does not happen. The other way in which a sheriff could have power to grant a warrant under the Official Secrets Act would be if some other Act of Parliament contained a general provision stating that JP should always be read as including sheriff, or stating that sheriffs should have all the powers, duties and functions of JPs. But Professor Robert Black, the distinguished head of the Department of Scots Law in the University of Edinburgh, and I have looked up every Act of Parliament under the headings dealing with the appointment, powers, duties and jurisdiction of JPs and sheriffs in Scotland. We can find no trace of a statutory provision to the effect that sheriffs are by virtue of their office JPs or should be deemed to be JPs or have the powers and responsibilities of JPs.

Lord Cameron, the Lord Advocate, the Attorney General for Scotland, has dismissed the claims that a sheriff is not qualified and asserted that a sheriff holds a judicial office senior to that of a Justice of the Peace and also possesses 'magisterial powers' under common law and statute in relation to the granting of warrants.

But how can the common law confer upon a sheriff powers which an Act of Parliament, in this case the Official Secrets Act, expressly provides shall be exercised by someone else, in this case a Justice of the Peace? Having talked to retired judges of the Appeal Court, and others in a position to know, I find that this constitutes an entirely novel and unprecedented legal concept.

Now it has been said by friends of the Government (though significantly not by Ministers) that these magisterial powers, or more precisely 'inherent powers of a sheriff', justify the police acting on the warrant. They contend that the effect of Section 288 of the Criminal Procedure (Scotland) Act of 1975, and the cases of Macpherson versus Boyd (1907) and Lawrence versus Ames (1921), is that a sheriff has inherent or implied power to perform any act that a statute says can be performed by a Justice of the Peace. This is fallacious. What the 1975 Act and the two cases do is to provide that if a statute grants to a lower court jurisdiction to try a particular type of offence, then the sheriff court, as a court of universal jurisdiction, also has inherent or implied jurisdiction to try that type of offence on the same terms and under the same conditions as would apply in the lower court. But, and it is a very big 'but' indeed, Section 9 of the Official Secrets Act does not concern jurisdiction to try Official Secrets offences. It deals solely with the question of granting search warrants in the course of the preliminary investigation of offences which are suspected but which have not yet resulted in the bringing of charges. In relation to *that* question, the provisions of Section 288 of the 1975 Act and

Macpherson versus Boyd and Lawrence versus Ames are wholly irrelevant. There is no authority that any of my legal friends can discover which permits a sheriff in that context to grant a warrant which Parliament had specifically stated should be granted by a Justice of the Peace.

This is not simply pedantry and legal nit-picking. Far deeper issues than technicalities are involved. A sheriff is a professional. He is responsible to the Lord Advocate, the Minister. A Justice of the Peace is a layman. My father was a Justice of the Peace. If he or thousands like him had been asked to sign a warrant to allow the police to go into the BBC, every alarm bell in his being would have rung. At the very least, he would have hesitated. He would have found friends, also JPs, to consult. I must have time to consider this, he would have said. And so would any sensible JP in Scotland of the present day.

But it was *time* that those who conducted the operation in London could not allow. Why the desperate urgency? The reason is easy to locate. By noon on Sunday 1 February, even senior members of Mrs Thatcher's Cabinet were on the telephone to Number Ten, asking what in heaven's name was happening in Broadcasting House in Glasgow. Foreseeably and foreseen, predictably and predicted, by the morning of Monday 2 February when the Court of Session in Edinburgh could have opened a calm and serious debate on what the BBC should hand to the police, the bemused silence of MPs, press and judges would not be assured in the way that it was likely to be guaranteed in the small hours of that Sunday morning.

Time was of the essence. So the law of Scotland was flouted by those who deployed the police. Had it not been flouted, the same people could not have achieved their objective of getting hold of the *Secret Society* programmes.

It may be said that the law should be different, that sheriffs should have powers to sign warrants in relation to the·Official Secrets Act. Maybe or maybe not. Maybe those who discussed the 1975 Act were unwilling to give these particular powers to a professional, and wanted a lay element introduced. On the other hand, they may have had no such foresights.

Yet it does not matter the proverbial tinker's cuss. All of us, in many fields, would like to have different laws, to fit in with our point of view. Perhaps we can persuade Parliament to make changes. But in the meantime, the law is the law is the law. And we have to abide by it. And no one has said this more often, or in more strident language, than Mrs Margaret Hilda Thatcher. She gives us this message daily. So I believe she and her minions should be made to stick to the law – even if it seems archaic and does not suit their own particular purposes of the moment.

When I asked Peter Fraser, the Solicitor General for Scotland, in the House on 11 March 1987, by what statutory provision or principle of the common law a sheriff has legal authority to grant a warrant that Parliament has specifically stated should be granted by someone else, he avoided the nub issue of legal authority, and used the occasion to berate me for a 'wholly unwarranted slur' against the sheriffs of Scotland[1] – when I had cast no slur at all on sheriffs singly or collectively. But then the Parliamentary smokescreen is an increasingly common Ministerial device.

This was only one encounter out of many during February and March when the Solicitor General simply ducked the question of legal authority. On 16 February I asked whether the Lord Advocate and local Procurator Fiscal were being kept informed by the police about progress into alleged breaches of the Official Secrets Act over 'Project Zircon'. Peter Fraser assured me that a full report was to be submitted by the police in due course. Yet by the time of writing, August 1987, no action looks like being forthcoming. For the simple reason, I would suggest, that any investigation into the identity of a mole would be fruitless. There never has been any mole to catch. Duncan Campbell relied on published knowledge, and on talking to the great and good like Sir Frank Cooper, Sir Ronald

---

[1] Hansard, cols 291–2.

Mason and indeed Sir Michael Havers with whom he had lunch on more than one occasion.

Here then is another evasion. On the same day I also asked why the Lord Advocate had failed to seek any kind of interdict on the publication of the material in the BBC programme as soon as he was aware that Duncan Campbell was likely to publish an article on the subject in the *New Statesman* of 23 January 1987. The Solicitor General's answer was uncharacteristically naïve. He claimed the Lord Advocate had 'no grounds for believing' there was a likelihood of publication. What did Government Ministers suppose Duncan Campbell would do with all his information?

And why did the Assistant Procurator Fiscal seek a warrant for material on the entire *Secret Society* series and not just for material on Project Zircon? The Written Answer came back that the 'highly classified' material was 'so interwoven that it was not possible immediately to disentangle one kind of material from another'. But the body set up by Government, the organisation brought into existence to cope with such precise problems, the D-Notice Committee, thought differently. The joint chairman of the Committee, Sir Clive Whitmore (incidentally also Permanent Secretary at the Ministry of Defence), was aware of the programmes, as was another member, Alan Protheroe. Yet the committee had made no move of its own to prevent their being shown.

If an MP wants to make a serious case, he can either write a book, or write an authoritative newspaper article, or in certain circumstances get an influential friend to set out his view in an article. Learning of his disquiet, I had phoned Anthony Bradley about his views. Secondhand, via me, a non-lawyer, these views would carry little weight, but set out under Bradley's own name, it would be a different kettle of fish. Sometime Fellow in Law of Trinity Hall, Cambridge, editor of *Public Law*, Professor of Constitutional Law in the University of Edinburgh, Anthony Bradley is not a man who can be dismissed on his own subject. The result was an article in the *Independent* on 11 February, in which Professor Bradley said it was 'not credible that the Lord Advocate could have properly performed his duties' in an apparent breach of official secrecy 'without informing himself as to the damage to the public interest caused by the Zircon film and the *Secret Society* series as a whole'. He went on to say that 'for this purpose his information must have come from those responsible for the intelligence and security services. At ministerial level, this would be the Foreign Secretary, as regards GCHQ, the Home Secretary who has general responsibility for the security services, the Defence Secretary, and the Prime Minister who has an overriding responsibility for security . . . Before he could properly have authorised the request for the warrant in Glasgow, the Lord Advocate would have had to be satisfied that the affair was so grave as to justify the wholesale search and seizure of the BBC's tapes and files.'

For me, as a politician, the *raison d'être* of having such an article is that it can be followed up. When did the Crown Office – the Lord Advocate's department – first approach or talk to the Foreign Office which was the major victim of the alleged breach? I asked the Solicitor General. At no time had the Crown Office contacted the Foreign Office, was his answer.

So by what alchemy did the noble lord, Lord Cameron of Lochbroom, on his 'tod' make such far-reaching decisions? I would like to say here, as I did in the Commons, that Kenny Cameron is a civilised and decent man, who has done a great deal of good in preserving the New Town of eighteenth- and nineteenth-century Edinburgh as chairman of the Cockburn Society. His father is a distinguished judge, and he himself was chosen as Lord Advocate because the Conservative hierarchy wanted someone who could command respect at Parliament House in Edinburgh. But Kenny Cameron would be the first to admit that he has never been elected by anyone to anything in public life. And yet, here we have him supposedly making a judgement on a highly political matter without reference to anyone among his colleagues. Impossible.

Other questions were asked. How had the Crown Office assessed the extent of the damage to national security? What steps had the Lord Advocate taken to satisfy himself of the adequacy of the search warrants? These and other enquiries were blocked by the time-honoured technique of giving references to previous Parliamentary proceedings which do not answer the questions asked.

The implications here do not simply involve the misuse of the Official Secrets Act. They also involve the issues of press freedom, the role of the police in the whole affair, and accountability to Parliament. The legal moves against the *New Statesman*, and against Duncan Campbell (as against Peter Wright) were taken late in the day. For more than six months, Government sources at the Foreign Office had known of the planned television programme. One explanation of the delay is that the Government suddenly alighted on a campaign to intimidate the BBC in an election year. What may, as a result, be under threat is the right to a free press and to impart information and ideas without interference by any public authority: a fundamental right.

The exact role of the Special Branch in the sorry business remains largely unexplained. Similar questions to those asked of the Crown Office must be put. Who directly or indirectly urged it to act, and with what instructions? These things do not happen by a process of spontaneous combustion. Someone, somewhere has to act as the catalyst. Who authorised the use of such widely drawn search warrants? Whenever such questions have been addressed to them, a succession of Ministers have gone to great pains to say, 'It wasn't me,' and wring their hands. As the *Glasgow Herald* put it on 3 February 1987: 'Clearly much more needs to be known about the mechanism used in initiating the raids . . . Yet whatever the Government's role in initiating the enquiry, and however far it can distance itself from the decision to adopt sledgehammer tactics, there must be ultimate political responsibility for the absurd yet sinister episode at Queen Margaret Drive.'

Consider the position of the Secretary of State for Scotland (the Home Secretary for Scotland, in other words), Malcolm Rifkind. On 11 February he said he was informed for the first time of the existence of a search warrant by Strathclyde Police officers at the BBC's Glasgow office when he arrived there on the evening of Friday 30 January. He claimed that though he was told there was likely to be a police operation there the following day, he was told nothing about the nature of that operation. Four days later he reiterated the claim.

Gordon Wilson, Chairman of the Scottish National Party, put the position neatly: 'I am sure he [Rifkind] knew perfectly well what was going to happen. I am sure that he got enough information about the nature of the inquiry, knew that the Prime Minister was behind the raid, and felt it would be injudicious to turn over the stone and see what was crawling underneath.' Mr Rifkind's attitude and lack of curiosity provoked these words in a letter of 14 February from me:

I'm puzzled. How can there have been such a lack of reaction, by someone such as yourself, who is a politician to your fingertips? A police raid on the BBC Office in Glasgow would be a matter of enormous political sensitivity. I cannot believe that – unless you knew a lot more from other sources – you simply shrugged your proverbial shoulders, and asked no further questions. Such a lack of curiosity would have been wholly out of keeping with all your previous known behaviour, and I find it reckless in an ambitious Cabinet Minister.

So, I put it to you – and will go on relentlessly asking, in one form or another, until the whole picture becomes clear, the following questions:

1. Did the Scottish Office official, who was informed by the police of the raid, tell you at the first opportunity? If not, why not? Did he or she take the view that such

a matter as a weekend search of the BBC could wait until Monday morning, and routine business?

As the police search, at moderated level, was the first item on the 1 p.m. news on Saturday 31 January – I phoned Chris Moncrieff with comments I was to make at Broxburn at 1.10 p.m. that afternoon – did this official still think that throughout the Saturday or Sunday that there was no need to contact his or her Secretary of State? The only likely explanation is that the official concerned knew by some means or another that he or she was expected to 'leave you alone', as it was all part of a pre-ordained plan.

2.   Since the official apparently did not tell you, is he or she to be rebuked or reprimanded?

Were there perhaps some 'misunderstandings between civil servants' of the kind with which we became so familiar during discussion of the Law Officer's letter on Westland?

I make it clear that I am not asking for action against your officials, as I find it distasteful when politicians blame civil servants in order to get out of a corner.

3.   Did the official or Scottish Office inform Number Ten, and your former Department, the Foreign Office, of the proposed police raid?

After all, so concerned was Geoffrey Howe with this very issue that he had cancelled a meeting with the miffed American envoy, Philip Habib, in order to concentrate on handling the Zircon affair. It is not as if the Foreign Office were uninterested in the matter, or regarded it as peripheral!

4.   If you say the official or Scottish Office did not see fit to pass on this information about a police raid to Number Ten, and the FCO, will you explain why they did not do so?

5.   You had every opportunity from 2 February until 13 February to say what you know, and when you knew it. So why wait until the information is dragged out of

you? Why does 11 days of controversy elapse before it is winkled from you that you knew in advance of police intentions? The *impression* was given – you will correct me if I am wrong about the impression – that you, like the Prime Minister, had first heard about the police raid on the radio.

His answer was little better than the proverbial lemon. His lack of curiosity went unexplained. Yet it was dragged out of him – shades of the process of extracting information in relation to the *Belgrano* – that a senior officer in the Police Division of the Scottish Home and Health Department was telephoned between 11 a.m. and 12 noon on Friday 30 January.

Was a wholesale raid on the BBC really a matter so trivial that the Secretary of State, let alone Downing Street, Mr Bernard Ingham, Uncle Tom Cobley and all should not be bothered? It beggars belief that the message was not passed up the line.

There can be only one interpretation for such mind-boggling lack of curiosity on the part of an ambitious, upwardly mobile Cabinet Minister – that he had been told, probably at Thursday Cabinet on 29 January, to keep his nose clean and out of the mess.

Subsequently, the answers to legitimate questions became terser and terser, stone-walls set up in order to gain time and create conditions whereby other matters engage public attention, and awkwardness vanish by boredom.

Unsurprisingly, other senior Cabinet Ministers have shown little appetite for having their names linked with the operation, among them Home Secretary Douglas Hurd. It was on Thursday 29 January that Metropolitan Police officers decided to seek the assistance of the Scottish authorities in procuring a search warrant for the BBC offices. I am told by three previous Home Secretaries that in their day they would have expected the Met. to have had more than a word with them about any such proposal. Douglas Hurd was not told because, being the man he is, he might well have objected. On 3 February, Hurd told the Commons, 'No Minister knew of the steps that the police were proposing in the course of their investigation.' This is palpably and provenly untrue. As we have seen, Malcolm Rifkind was told on Friday 30 January.

Even more anxious not to become involved or even associated with what had happened was the ex-Secretary of State for Scotland, the Member of Parliament for Ayr, one of Mrs Thatcher's putative successors as leader of the Tory Party, the present Secretary of State for Defence George Younger. At endless meetings with the Foreign Secretary and others, he made sure that Zircon was a Foreign Office responsibility, as the Foreign Office are responsible for GCHQ. Then, with ill-concealed relief, Mr Younger sped off to Saudi Arabia to sell them more arms, making himself scarce when the storm was at its height.

Less fortunate was the Foreign Secretary. So consumed was Sir Geoffrey Howe with the implications of Zircon, according to a senior lobby correspondent, that he had to ask his junior to go and read the speech he would have made to an important meeting of the Middle East Association (when Beirut was headline news), and, without any precedent I can find, cancel at short notice a scheduled meeting with the American special envoy, Philip Habib. But then, for Mrs Thatcher and her Ministers, political embarrassment at home always takes priority over our country's international relations.

The Foreign Office was the prime victim and firmly wedged into the strategy. To quote Professor Bradley in the *Independent*, 'As a matter of expediency, the public prosecutor in Scotland, in deciding upon the mode and style of an investigation, must often take into account the wishes of the victim of that offence.' The FCO's feelings were indeed very much taken into account. Naturally and properly they did consult with Downing Street.

As to Sir Michael Havers, who ought to have been up to the neck in any such escapade, he was kept blissfully unaware, being regarded by the prime movers as somewhat detached from the present Government. (They cannot, alas, do the simple thing and sack him because he knows too much about their misdeeds during the Westland affair.) So he, happily, did not know anything until Sunday 1 February.

Most difficult of all, perhaps, was the position of the BBC, not least because the raid happened (by chance?) during a period of interregnum, when Alasdair Milne had departed and Michael Checkland had not yet been appointed. Seven BBC employees, including the assistant Director General and the Controller of the BBC in Scotland, were questioned at length about the BBC's internal documents. Each interrogation lasted an average of five hours. In early March, BBC Scotland's public oversight body, the Broadcasting Council for Scotland, urged the Corporation to take action to defend its staff against such continued 'harassment' by the police. Senior staff are profoundly unhappy, and none more so than the assistant Director General Alan Protheroe.

For at stake, among other considerations, was the BBC's international reputation. Abroad, headlines such as 'Thatcher gags broadcasters' abounded. The European Parliament voted in support of a motion of condemnation.

At the time of writing, August 1987, the BBC position is that they are still examining the legal advice they have received. If nothing significant is found by the police as a result of the raid, I believe that litigation would serve a purpose in helping to resolve the numerous legal obscurities attaching to the warrant and to the raid. I know that these considerations have not escaped the BBC's legal advisers, including the Dean of the Faculty of Advocates. In the *Glasgow Herald* of 25 February 1987 it was reported that the Dean of Faculty had advised the BBC that the warrant was not obtained by the proper procedure; that it was invalid; and that there were good grounds for raising an action for damages.

Alas, the coyness of the BBC about testing their position in court has little to do with the legal basis, and more to do with the politics of broadcasting and their relationship with the Prime Minister. And it is to Mrs Thatcher's role we must now turn.

The Strathclyde Police did not move, as the Prime Minister would have us believe, like self-directed robots, beyond all Government reach and influence. Nor, for that matter, did the Metropolitan Police. I believe to this day what I was originally told: that the action against Queen Margaret Drive was carried out 'with the authority of Number Ten Downing Street'. Now I do not claim that they were told that it was done with the authority of Mrs Thatcher. Because, as one former mandarin of the Civil Service put it to me succinctly, 'But, Tam, she may indeed have given instructions that as Prime Minister she was *not* to be told details.' Especially after the Law Officer's letter in the Westland affair, she would have been most careful not to be up front herself. But it was the old Henry II and Becket syndrome once again. 'Who will rid me of Duncan Campbell and all his programmes?' A far cry from the occasion when Reggie Bevins, the working-class Tory Postmaster-General, was goaded by reporters into saying that he would 'do something about *That-Was-The-Week-That-Was*' lampooning the then Prime Minister. On his desk, the following morning, there was a simple note: 'Reggie. Oh no, you won't! Harold [Macmillan].'

Mrs Thatcher instructed her press secretary, Bernard Ingham, to tell the press that the first she had heard of it all was on the radio the same evening (Saturday 31 January 1987). I believe this is egregious Prime Ministerial nonsense, as would anyone who was acquainted with the contemporary machinery and personnel inside Number Ten. In fact, so concerned were she and her Government with this affair of Zircon that, as we have seen, they had been forced to snub an American envoy. A topic which was the cause of Prime Minister, Foreign Secretary and Defence Secretary being closeted together for hours on end was not going to be left to the Crown Office in Edinburgh, one of the most remote Government Departments and headed by political innocents, to do as it thought fit.

The Prime Minister then had the bland effrontery to answer my question as to why her Home Secretary asserted that no Minister knew, and why he stuck to that position when the Scottish Secretary confessed that he was told before the event, with a non-sequitur.[1]

A Minister *did* know of the steps that the police were proposing in the course of their investigation. And his Scottish Office knew. And if only to protect themselves, they made jolly sure that the lead Department, the Foreign Office, knew. And they made sure that via the Foreign Office, Downing Street knew. No one in official Scotland surmised for one moment that a raid on the BBC was a matter so trivial that Mr Bernard Ingham would not care to be informed about it. If senior civil servants at the Scottish Office and Crown Office seemed officially relaxed, it was because they were given to understand that it was Downing Street's policy, and therefore no wrath would descend on them or their Ministers. In their private capacity, some good men and women, faithful officials of successive Governments of different colours, have let it be known round Edinburgh that they are appalled and angry.

At school, I won a prize for Latin construe – and had I known that I would become a Member of Parliament, I

---

[1] Parliamentary Question 98 of 20 February 1987, answered by the Prime Minister on 23 February:

Mr Tam Dalyell: To ask the Prime Minister if, in view of the Right honourable Member for Witney's statement of 3rd February, Official Report, column 823, and subsequent statement by the Right honourable Member for Edinburgh Pentlands, she will take measures to improve co-ordination between Ministers in respect of information relating to the police raid on the British Broadcasting Corporation in Queen Margaret Drive.

The Prime Minister: My Right hon. Friends the Members for Witney and Edinburgh Pentlands have made it clear that they have no role in the conduct of police investigations or the obtaining of search warrants.

might have made arrangements to do my degree in philology. On 5 March 1987, Mrs Thatcher told me that 'There is no evidence that press officers from any Government Department other than the Scottish Office have been in contact with Strathclyde Police at any stage about the action of the BBC.' True, there may be no evidence. But that is because Downing Street took jolly good care not to leave its fingerprints on the operation of which it was the godfather. Contact there certainly was – at one remove.

When the Prime Minister was asked if she would refer to the Security Commission[1] the question of the 'disclosure of information' to Duncan Campbell, she kicked for touch. 'While the police investigation into this matter is in progress, it would be premature to consider whether a referral to the Security Commission is appropriate.' If the Prime Minister's purposes had been genuine concern about national security, such a referral would have been made many moons ago, and by Prime Ministerial statement in the House.

But what she said in the House was revealing. I listened to the woman, more like a fishwife than a Prime Minister, yattering shrilly on about 'people anxious to ferret out' state secrets 'for personal gain'. The answer to this is that the real breeders of Parliamentary ferrets are those who lie to the Commons about matters in which the motive is their supposed political gain, rather than the real interests of Britain.

The Prime Minister claimed on 17 February that 'Ministers have made clear repeatedly in the House that the Government did not intervene in the application for a warrant to search the premises of the BBC in Glasgow'. Yes, but they had no need to intervene; for they had instigated it.

[1] Chairman: Law Lord, Lord Griffiths; Deputy Chairman: Mr Justice, Sir Anthony Lloyd; members: Lord Allen of Abbeydale (former Permanent Secretary at the Home Office), General Sir Hugh Beach, Sir Alan Cottrell, Sir Michael Palliser, and Air Chief Marshal Sir Alasdair Steadman.

This Prime Minister's purpose was to teach the BBC a lesson. To create a climate in an election year when the major broadcasting network was unwilling to challenge the Government. Mrs Thatcher claims that she wants to roll back the State. In terms of freedom of expression, she is rolling on the State. Thanks to Robin Cook MP, Parliamentary colleagues were given the opportunity to see the banned films, and an unlikely combination of Tony Benn, Enoch Powell, and former Prime Minister Sir James Callaghan defeated Mrs Thatcher's motion to have the House of Commons ban itself from seeing material the Government had managed to ban elsewhere. If passed, such a motion would have been a remarkable curtailment of the rights of the House. Fortunately, it rose to the occasion and Party divisions were, for an historic moment, set aside. It was a galling experience for Mrs Thatcher, no less so for being uncommon in these last nine years.

I believe that with Mrs Thatcher pique and temper can be the father and mother of policy. Thwarted by the House of Commons, and learning that the raid on the *New Statesman* had yielded little or nothing, Henry II-like word went out from Downing Street to seize the BBC's films – all of them in the series. Some seventy-two hours later, in Glasgow, her wishes were obeyed. The MP for the constituency, Roy Jenkins, dubbed it the work 'of a second-rate police state'. If this chapter started with a quotation from the Conservative *Glasgow Herald*, let it end with the words of an American President, Thomas Woodrow Wilson, who always extolled the virtues of 'pitiless publicity for public business'.

6

Economical With the Truth

The first occasion on which I am conscious of having heard the name of Peter Wright was when I came in from the terrace of the House of Commons to avoid a summer shower of rain, and went up to see a Parliamentary friend in the Opposition Whips' Office. The television was on. It was Monday 16 July, 1984. Coming in at the middle of a *World in Action* programme, I looked at the screen and became more and more curious, as one sometimes does even when one has missed the beginning of a programme.

'Those of us intimately involved in the Hollis investigation,' said an elderly gentleman on the screen, 'believed that Hollis had been a long-term Soviet penetration agent in MI5.' 'Who's this?' I asked my friend, who was the London area Whip. 'Some geezer, Tam,' came the illuminating reply.

The interviewer then said, 'Why do you think then that Mrs Thatcher didn't square that with Parliament?' 'Because,' said Mr Peter Wright, for it was he who was the geezer, 'she was advised by the security service, who were anxious that there shouldn't be a high-level independent enquiry into the service that might drag skeletons out of the cupboard that they would not want to be revealed.' For the rest of the programme, in some detail and recalling at length the case of the Russian Embassy clerk in Ottawa in 1946, Igor Gouzenko, Wright made his now familiar case against the late Sir Roger Hollis.

Thus for half an hour, at peak viewing time, Peter Wright drove a coach and four through the idea that former employees of the security services should not discuss their experiences. And it was the vivid if blurred memory of this programme, and the circumstances in which I watched it in the Opposition Whips' Office, which sparked off the deep scepticism I have felt, and shown, from the moment the Government decided to prosecute Peter Wright in an Australian court.

In the *Guardian* of 11 December 1986 a senior journalist, Richard Norton-Taylor, quotes Sir Robert Armstrong at the trial in Sydney as maintaining that the Government did not know about the Granada *World in Action* programme until the day before it went out. Sir Robert Armstrong is wrong. The Government knew for weeks in advance. As Mr Justice Powell said in his judgment of 13 March 1987, 'Despite its being forwarned of the preparation and intended televising of the programme, it would seem that the Service took no steps to attempt to ascertain the content of the proposed programme and it is, in any event, clear that the British Government took no steps to attempt to stop the programme being televised.' (As we saw in the last chapter, the Government were equally warned – by Professor Ronald Mason and Sir Frank Cooper, who themselves took part in the programme – about the content of the 'Zircon' programme months before it was due to be screened. But they did nothing at a time when they could have done something if they had pleased, or been really concerned about national security rather than playing politics.)

As we shall find, however, there were skeletons in the cupboard, though rather different skeletons from those which Peter Wright had in mind. What haunted the Prime Minister had little to do with the security of Britain, and everything to do with Mr Wright's description of bugging and burgling his way through London in the 1970s, during the time of Harold Wilson's Government. As the *Sunday Times* of 23 November 1986 had it: 'Whitehall officials who have read Wright's book say that they went "cross-eyed" when they came to the passages dealing with Wilson. One official says that Wright claims that MI5 were responsible for a series of burglaries and buggings at Wilson's homes and offices . . . in an effort to discover whether Wilson or his close advisers were communists or even Soviet agents.'

One of the Prime Minister's main motives in launching the prosecution of Wright stemmed from the frenetic pressure of MI5. If Wright's revelations were to be made public, officials feared that a future Labour Government would be tempted to purge or even disband the existing Intelligence services and start afresh. This neither the cosily anti-Labour world of MI5 nor Mrs Thatcher wished.

The American press across the United States carried the following Reuter report: 'Labor MP Tam Dalyell said he would challenge Prime Minister Margaret Thatcher to say when she learned of the extent of the operations against Wilson. "It now seems clear that the Government's legal action is intended to prevent details of the surveillance of the Wilson Government from becoming public."' Labour backbenchers do not normally make the *New York Times*, the *Washington Post*, and the *Los Angeles Times*, unless it is thought that they have something to say.

There is a very respectable case to be deployed against the thesis that we all have an absolute right to know absolutely everything. In my view, contrary to that of some of my best political friends, we do not and should not have any such right. Nor should ex-employees of the State, working in the security services, believe that it is acceptable to break their oaths of confidence, and then say on television or publish what they will, either for money, or to advance their own views or their vendettas against former colleagues, alive or dead. Reluctantly, I concede that the nation needs a secret service, and that it needs to know that its activities will remain secret.

So it might have followed that I should be shouting from the rooftops that the Government was correct to attempt to stop Peter Wright from breaching not only the Official Secrets Act, but also commonly held views of confidentiality and commonly held standards of right and wrong. And in fact I might well have said openly that it was necessary to prosecute Peter Wright *pour décourager les autres* – but for one thing, namely the aforementioned television programme. What conceivable logic is there in doing nothing about a television programme featuring an ex-employee of the security services, seen by eight million people plus, and then making a mountain out of a relative molehill by attempting to stop his memoirs being published? None whatsoever.

The paramount point about having a secret service is that *all* its personnel should be of the highest possible calibre. And here I must voice my extreme concern. During my National Service in the Army in Germany, I formed a rather favourable impression of the Military Intelligence personnel. But that was in 1950–52. Some fifteen years later I had my next encounter. I was asked to go and see a man in the Ministry of Defence building. The meeting turned out to involve questions as to what I knew about a particular lady who might be a security risk in relation to the Soviet Union. I could not believe my ears. I was being questioned about a scatter-brained West Lothian worthy who had been all round the political shop; within the space of two years she had been a member of the Labour Party, the Conservative Party, the Communist Party, and the Scottish National Party. The notion that she could be of value to the KGB was simply preposterous.

For confirmation that such incompetence is not an isolated example, one need only remind oneself of the Bettaney case. Bettaney was arrested in London in September 1983. His recruitment to MI5's sensitive 'K' branch, dealing with counter-espionage, was inexplicable. As a disturbed Oxford undergraduate, Bettaney had veered from neo-Nazi to Marxist beliefs. His alcohol problems were well known to his colleagues in MI5. But it was only after the Soviets grew sick and tired of his approaches to them, and informed MI5 on purpose, that Bettaney was investigated. He was jailed for twenty-three years.

What on earth was a man of the known record and behaviour of Bettaney doing in the security services? It was a farce and a disgrace. Nor do I have a high opinion at all of most of those Conservative MPs who have in recent years been associated with the security services. I say in recent years because I do have a high opinion of some of those in an older generation, such as Julian Amery and the late Neil Marten – and I am one who freely admits to friendship with and personal regard for many Conservative MPs, even where there are enormous political differences.

Clive Ponting, who had to work with MI5 officials when he headed the Ministry of Defence's legal secretariat, says that he found MI5 staff he met to be far to the Right: 'They're utterly reactionary, tucked away in their little world of their own.' From other sources I have found corroboration for his view that they are well to the right of the British political spectrum. Nor did Ponting find any evidence of individual Ministerial control of the security services, through the Ministry of Defence or anywhere else in Whitehall: 'Essentially, what they don't choose to tell the Prime Minister, the Prime Minister cannot know about. It all works on the traditional Whitehall assumption that there are reasonable men in charge.'

When I was the guest of the Islwyn Constituency Labour Party at their Chartist Rally in November 1985, I devoted most of my speech to telling the Chairman for the evening that he had to grasp the nettle. 'If they were like that with Harold,' I said to him, 'think what they're going to be like with you, Neil.' That is one of the sentiments which haunts me, and prompted this chapter and this book. I shall not forget how the security services managed to mistake my friend and Parliamentary neighbour Judith Hart, in 1974, for a Mrs Tudor Hart who had been a communist until 1956.

When politicians mount their high horses in public,

invoking this sacred principle or that, it is wise to sup with a long spoon. Whatever else it was about, the decision to go to the court in New South Wales was emphatically not about the abstract principle of security service personnel identifying themselves, and going public on their experiences. Otherwise the Government would have taken steps, for it had warning, to stop the *World in Action* programme of July 1984. Nor can we believe that the despatch of the Cabinet Secretary to the other side of the world was simply in order to protect the memory of the late Sir Roger Hollis. Personally, I have never believed that Sir Roger Hollis was a spy. But whether he was or wasn't, whether certain eminent persons wanted or did not want to bury their own guilty feelings in the bones of Sir Roger Hollis, is immaterial. It would be romantic and whimsical, to a degree that Mrs Thatcher's administration is not, to propel the Cabinet Secretary to the Antipodes on a mission impossible, simply to uphold the maxim of '*De mortuis nil nisi bonum*'.

Nor are Peter Wright's memoirs seen as a threat to the national security of our country. As the judge in the Sydney court suggested, Mr Wright's outpourings had a good deal in common with *Boys' Own* and Biggles:

> While, when discussing technological questions, Mr Wright provides information which would, no doubt, be of interest to the lay reader, such detail as is provided seems to me as if it would be of not the slightest use to a technician, even if – which it is not – the technology being discussed was contemporary, and had not been discussed in other books which have been published over the years; second, that when, in the course of his manuscript, Mr Wright discusses 'non-technical operations', he does so in a style which, to me, seems more appropriate to 'The Boys' Own Paper' or 'Biggles' Flying Omnibus' rather than to an arid scholarly work recording the detail, and analysing the success or otherwise, of covert security or intelligence operations.

For the real reason for the novel behaviour of a British Government in sending their Cabinet Secretary to do that which he ought not to have accepted doing, in the view of some of his retired peers such as Lord Bancroft, we must look elsewhere. As usual, the ignition of the Government's action had nothing to do with security, and one proverbial heck of a lot to do with political embarrassment. As Gerald Kaufman, the Shadow Home Secretary, said, 'The humiliation that Mrs Thatcher has forced on Sir Robert Armstrong has inflicted grave harm on the security services. They are being exposed not only to needless publicity but to damaging ridicule as well. Yet the Prime Minister's cries of "security" are a fig leaf which conceals the real issue for Parliament. The questions to be answered in the Commons are not about security, but about the extraordinary and inconsistent conduct of Mrs Thatcher and the Attorney General.'[1]

Because of the Government's embarrassment, a civil servant was used for a task that ought to have been carried out by an elected politician. Media comment has portrayed Sir Robert Armstrong as some kind of a fool in the Australian court. But from the chapter on Westland, we know that a fool he is not. A man who so skilfully stonewalled in the spring of 1986, with a display of verbal pyrotechnics the like of which I have hardly ever heard before a Select Committee, is unlikely to have changed character by the autumn of the same year. Yet, in the biting language of Mr Justice Powell, Sir Robert gave hearsay evidence, and he 'would not stoop to lie when a half-truth would do . . . I have to say that Sir Robert dissembled on one occasion, and I have to bear that in mind when I look at the rest of the evidence.'

I suspect, incidentally, that both Mrs Thatcher and Sir Robert Armstrong were lulled into a sense of false security by the way in which Sir Robert was perceived to have triumphed over the Select Committee. The style in which

[1] Speech of 23 November 1986.

he batted against the Select Committee's bowling led them to surmise that they had nothing to fear from an Australian courtroom. That was a mistake. It is as if Sir Robert, in London at the Oval, faced an over from Dilley, followed by an over from Old, followed by an over from Cowan, followed by one from Small, followed by a succession of spinners, one over each. To pursue the analogy, at the Sydney courtroom he was facing hostile, sustained bowling from a Lillee and a Thomson. As Bruce Anderson, feature writer of the *Sunday Telegraph*, observed, 'it is much easier to hold off a number of MPs, few of them trained interrogators, all fighting for air space and interrupting each other's arguments, than a single battle-hardened counsel'.

Mrs Thatcher bounced Sir Robert Armstrong into a task which he did not want, which was none of his business, which was a perversion of the age-old constitutional niceties, and which he knew from an early stage was a certain loser. Mrs Thatcher sent him in the full glare of worldwide publicity to defend a case which was indefensible.

I believe that in thirty or fifty years' time, depending on the Public Record Office rules of the day, we will learn that Sir Robert minuted the Prime Minister that Sir Michael Havers, the Attorney General, was the right man for the witness box. The Prime Minister's excuse, real or politically motivated, was that Sir Michael's health was at risk, and she shamed Sir Robert into accepting. What should he have done? Civil servants are often overruled by politicians and told to get on with things of which they do not approve. Fair enough. That is democracy, when it relates to policy.

It is a rather different matter when, as very occasionally happened in the past but is happening again under Mrs Thatcher, they are instructed to do things that are clearly, to them and their Civil Service colleagues, unconstitutional or unethical. The instructions to Sir Robert Armstrong came into the latter category. As Sir Robert may have wanly recollected, Colette Bowe, the DTI press secretary who was 'ordered to leak' during the Westland affair, faced the same problem. No one knew this better since it was Sir Robert himself who conducted the investigation. When Clive Ponting leaked the *Belgrano* information to me without authority, while serving in the Ministry of Defence, Sir Robert was prompted to opine that Ponting ought to have knocked on his door. But on whose door was Sir Robert to knock? Was he to go and knock on his own door and tell himself that he had a grievance against the Prime Minister for asking him to do something that was unethical? On top of Ponting, Tisdall and Bowe, this completes the case for having the kind of body to whom Service personnel, police officers like John Stalker, and civil servants can go if they think that they are being abused. In the wake of these cases, the Civil Service has made it clear that officials faced with dubious instructions have the right to take their unease upwards. But for the head of the Civil Service, there is nowhere else to go when he is the one with the problem. I am told that Sir Robert did seriously contemplate resignation, and decided against it.

The sagest advice to Sir Robert Armstrong came from his erstwhile political chief at the Home Office, Roy Jenkins. Among Mrs Thatcher's habits, said the new Chancellor of Oxford University,

> is her extraordinary capacity to expose to danger, and perhaps even to mutilation beyond hope of recovery, those who are closely associated with her. To some extent this applies to Ministers, as we can see from the case of the right hon. and learned Member for Richmond, Yorkshire (Mr Brittan), but I am concerned, not with Ministers, but with civil servants. Sir Robert Armstrong, as the Prime Minister must know well, should never have been sent to Australia, but it is not only he. Private secretaries and press officers are treated like junior officers, constantly called upon to go over the top in a desperate partisan assault not made more attractive by the fact that the Prime Minister's orders

are to safeguard the political life of their colonel-in-chief, the Prime Minister. My advice to the substantial number of notable civil servants who worked with or for me is, 'Do not get too close to this Prime Minister. She is a upas-tree – the branches may be splendid, but contact may be deadly.'[1]

The onus must rest not with Sir Robert, but with the Prime Minister who sent him. Only a remarkably narrow person would have requested an official to go. First of all, any one of us who has been to Australia (and I have) could have forecast that the Australians would wish to debunk the official British. It was also clear that they would regard the presence of any official, as opposed to politician, as patronising. The European editor of the *Australian Financial Review*, P. P. McGuiness, put the problem in true Australian style in a letter to the *Independent* when he said, 'The eager subservience of British judges to the government in this matter has been appalling . . . it also reveals that government's contempt for Australian courts, in that it was prepared to send its chief office boy to give hearsay evidence in the expectation that he would be believed.'[2]

Faced with questioning by reporters in Australia, Sir Robert Armstrong said, 'I don't know why I was selected for this job.' I think that could be translated as meaning, 'I know very well why I was selected for this job by the Prime Minister, and I'm getting fed up with what she has done to me. I am not appearing as a very likeable character, and my facility with words, which is admirable in Whitehall and in the Athenaeum, creates, I know too well, an impression of vanity and arrogance. I should never have agreed to the Prime Minister's request in the first place and am now kicking myself for having acquiesced in obliging her.'

[1] Hansard, 3 December 1986, col. 957.
[2] Letter of 14 March 1987.

Do not suppose for one moment that the Cabinet Secretary was cast adrift on Australia's legal waters, left alone without help and expected to survive as best he could. This would be far from the reality. Before the Cabinet Secretary was sent to Sydney, he was briefed, briefed, and re-briefed about the case for hours on end. He was supplied with papers, advised by the Government's most expert available lawyers, and given as much Prime Ministerial time as he asked for, to cover as many contingencies as possible.

In Australia, he could be and was in daily contact with the Cabinet Office and Downing Street. What he was saying in court was, with perhaps a little poetic licence, what it was agreed he could say. That is what puts a serious complexion on his misleading the court on the role of Sir Michael Havers, the Attorney General. He was repeating what could only have been the agreed position of the Government on the matters in question. The truth only came out because Sir Michael Havers in London insisted on denying that he had been consulted about instigating proceedings against Chapman Pincher to block publication of his book *Their Trade Is Treachery*. Sir Robert had to apologise for misleading the court by saying, wrongly, that legal advice he had been given had come from Sir Michael (who was the office-holder in whose name the Wright case was brought). It is symptomatic of this Government's pathological disdain for the truth that it knew of Sir Robert's false testimony concerning Sir Michael as soon as it was given and certainly no later than 20 November when Neil Kinnock first raised it in the House of Commons, and yet it took over a week before Sir Robert Armstrong put the record straight.

It was Neil Kinnock's exchange with the Prime Minister on 27 November which finally brought matters to a head:

Mr Kinnock: 'Will the Prime Minister tell us, was the decision not to impede publication of Mr Pincher's book in 1981 taken personally by the Attorney-General, and was the decision to put Sir Robert Armstrong in court in Australia taken personally by the Attorney-General?'

The Prime Minister: 'As I said to the House last Thursday, it would be inappropriate for me – [HON. MEMBERS: "Answer, answer"] – to comment on matters which may arise in the proceedings concerning the Peter Wright case in Australia while those proceedings continue.'[1]

Kinnock asked the Prime Minister to give a straight answer to a straight question. Had the Attorney General been a fool or a fall guy? Mrs Thatcher blocked again. The Leader of the Opposition then asked:

Mr Kinnock: 'The Prime Minister must, then, now explain what is the inference for national security of telling us whether it was an individual member of her Government who personally – not nominally and formally but personally – took a decision that has a direct effect on the integrity of national security in this country.'

The Prime Minister: 'The Government, as the right hon. Gentleman knows, are indivisible. *[Interruption.]* The decisions are decisions of the Government and not of particular Ministers. If he wishes to table a motion of censure, he is fully entitled to do so.'[2]

Only after this answer, which Peter Wright's defence lawyer correctly interpreted as meaning that Havers had *not* taken the decision on his own, did the Cabinet Secretary, the following day, admit that he had misled the court in Sydney. 'I am afraid,' he said, 'that I assumed from what I had been told that it [the Pincher case] had been referred to the Attorney personally. I now understand that it was not referred to the Attorney personally.'

Let us leave Sir Robert Armstrong's disingenuousness aside. Sir Michael Havers was kept in the dark about the Government's decision not to prevent *Their Trade Is*

[1] Hansard, cols 426–7.
[2] Ibid.

Treachery being published. I suspect he was kept in the dark about a green light being given, after legal exchanges, to Rupert Allason, alias Nigel West, for his book *A Matter of Trust*. And I know, because the Attorney General himself told me, at the entrance to the House of Commons, that he was kept in the dark about the subsequent volte-face by the Government in its decision to prosecute Peter Wright for his book *Spycatcher*.

What conclusions must we draw?

The first is that Mrs Thatcher's Government, far from being 'indivisible', as she claimed, works in a centralised, not to say secretive, way. Her former Foreign Secretary Francis Pym supports this view with feeling in his recent book *The Politics of Consent* when he says, 'Logic is being abandoned. A Government that set out with a mission to decentralise and to roll back the frontiers of the state is, in many respects, doing the precise opposite. The motive behind it is the belief that only by doing everything itself can the Government implement its policies, which is dangerously close to saying that the state always knows best.'[1]

The second and perhaps more crucial conclusion is that there may be some implication in Peter Wright's book that goes far beyond the day-to-day skulduggery, legal and illegal, that spies and spymasters get up to, which Mrs Thatcher has decided must be suppressed. I want to return to this. For now, the point is one of Governmental honesty. If Sir Michael Havers, then the Attorney General, was being kept up to date about issues involving possible breaches of official secrecy and possible illegality at the highest levels, one has a guarantee that Governmental probity was being observed and that improper conduct by Government servants – including the security services – would have been dealt with if it was discovered. If he was not, one has no such guarantee. Mrs Thatcher claimed to have MI5 under control, and what I have said may be the

[1] Hamish Hamilton, 1984.

idlest speculation. But in that case, why did she not set up an official inquiry into the story of the Wilson buggings, via a Select Committee or the Security Commission? And why *was* Sir Michael Havers kept in the dark?

Alan Williams MP, then Deputy Shadow Leader of the House, was moved to put it this way on 23 November 1986. 'If I were the Attorney General, I would be feeling extremely vulnerable. Number Ten used Leon Brittan as a body shield at the time of Westland, and now it looks as if the Attorney General has been nominated as the sacrificial lamb over the MI5 scandal.'

But it should be borne in mind that Sir Michael is for all practical purposes unsackable. He knows far too much about the Prime Minister's role in the Westland affair to be sacked unceremoniously against his will. What Sir Michael's denial that he had been consulted about blocking Pincher's book did, was to transfer the blame to where it really belonged – the door of Number Ten Downing Street. He made sure that in history, at all events, the buck should be seen to stop with Mrs Thatcher.

In previous times, it would have been bad enough if on one major occasion, such as Westland, the position of the Attorney General had been traduced. But, with the denial of his supposed role, for the second time within ten months, Sir Michael's position as the Government's legal adviser has been again traduced. For the second time, Sir Michael Havers has found it necessary to show that, as the mud begins to fly in all directions, he at least has clean hands. For the senior Law Officer to have been compelled to distance himself from the Government he serves is almost unheard-of: to have to do it twice within a year, on two separate issues, is surely without historical parallel.

Back in February 1986, I suggested that he did not resign only because such an action might have proved a mortal blow to a Government which was already reeling from the loss of a couple of Cabinet Ministers, and would certainly have destroyed the Prime Minister. By November and December 1986 the paramount consideration was once again not to cripple the Government. In days gone by when honourable behaviour was of surpassing importance for leading Conservative politicians, the revelations in London and in Sydney could hardly have been more serious. That they were shrugged off tells us a lot about the political morality of our day.

The passages in Wright's book which most worried Mrs Thatcher, when brought to her attention by Intelligence advisers such as Sir Anthony Duff, were not, as we have seen, those arguing that a former head of MI5 was a Soviet agent. No, that was a matter on which the Prime Minister was relaxed – before her time. What caused the real flutter in the dovecotes of Downing Street was something altogether more alarming: the passages covering illegal acts by MI5, including the investigation in the mid-1970s by a number of senior MI5 officers into Harold Wilson and members of Wilson's so-called 'kitchen cabinet'.

Wright's claim, that elements in MI5 were so worried about the Prime Minister that colleagues of his decided they had to investigate, is not one that he goes into in much detail in his book, I am told. He does not name the MI5 officers who were involved in the burglaries and buggings. Though I understand that MI5 knows the names of the team, no prosecutions are likely, despite illegal acts having been committed. Wright's personal position is that he refused to participate in the conspiracy and eventually reported it to a superior. But one opinion, quoted in the *Sunday Times* earlier this year, suggests that Wright did not want to say too much about the actions against the Wilson Government 'because *he* led all these operations'.[1]

If Peter Wright does not want to say too much about these operations, I certainly will from the position of a ringside seat.

My concerns pre-date the 1970s. I lived then, when in

[1] 23 November 1986.

London, in the house of Dick Crossman at 9 Vincent
Square. Between 1963 and 1966, virtually every Tuesday
to Thursday morning, George Wigg would phone – 'Wigg,
here,' the low quiet voice would say – and the calls were
seldom less than twenty minutes. George Wigg, the
Paymaster General, with whom I had an up-and-down
relationship, was obsessed with security. It was after one
of these lengthy calls – I dread to think how much Prime
Ministerial time George Wigg consumed in those days, as
he was on to Wilson before he was on to Crossman – that
Dick Crossman expatiated on a strange tale.

In June 1965 (I have checked my spasmodic diary)
Crossman told me about a conversation he had had with
Gerald Gardiner, his old Labour Party friend and QC who
had been made Labour Lord Chancellor. Gerald had said
that whenever he wanted to talk to Elwyn Jones, the
Attorney General, he would ask Elwyn to accompany him
on a car tour of Green Park. He explained that he did this
because he suspected MI5 of bugging the telephones in his
office. Gardiner himself repeated the story in the *Sunday
Times* in 1986: 'When I had to speak to the Attorney
General in confidence, I took him out in the car because
I knew the driver, and I knew she would never have
allowed the car to be bugged without my knowledge.'[1]
Crossman's attitude was characteristically cool, along the
lines of, 'What on earth should we expect other than to be
interfered with?' But this was ten years before the full-scale
operation mounted by Wright and his colleagues.

I am not impressed by the palliative, peddled in some
quarters, that it was simply a bunch of high-jinks MI5
officers, dashing around London, doing a series of covert
jobs on Harold Wilson and his inner circle of advisers. I
understand that Peter Wright refers to some forty MI5
officers engaged in the anti-Wilson activities (excluding
support staff). Is it possible that forty MI5 officers somehow detach themselves from their normal activities without

[1] 16 November 1986.

anybody's noticing? Candidly, I believe the entire 'high-jinks'/'small right-wing element' theory is one of the fall-back positions of explanation prepared by MI5 itself and its supporters. I have considerable respect on these matters for Jonathan Aitken, Conservative MP for Thanet South, whom I heard say in the House on 15 December 1986, 'It is almost inconceivable that any operation of the kind that seems to have been alleged could have been carried out on a completely unauthorised freelance basis.' I accept that Peter Wright's cronies may not have had formal or official authorisation for what they supposedly did, but equally the operation could not have taken place by spontaneous combustion. If it happened as Wright said it did, it must have happened with the tacit consent of senior MI5 officers.

Mrs Thatcher's attitude is to distance herself from such allegations. As in the Zircon affair, she has learned to operate at one remove. None of this is anything to do with her. In which case, why is she being so coy about authorising an investigation? Just this. In the 1970s there was an anti-Labour activity which it would even now be embarrassing to exhume, because exhuming it could mean bringing to light a far from effective, or politically impartial, secret service.

Let us digress from Peter Wright for a moment to touch on another sinister happening of the 1970s which has never been satisfactorily solved. I am referring to Ted Short and the case of the forged Swiss bank account.[1]

[1] The background can be succinctly put. Shortly after I was elected to the Commons in 1962, I had a 10-minute-rule Bill on the activities of a certain firm of money-lenders, then operating in Scotland. I said that a number of my constituents were suffering from usury, the like of which we had not 'seen since the khalifs of ancient Baghdad'. Ted Short, then Opposition Deputy Chief Whip, had constituents in Central Newcastle who suffered from the same firm. This brought us together, and though I drove him to distraction from time to time (particularly over devolution, where he was the Minister nominally in charge), he and I have remained firm friends ever since. It was natural, therefore, that in December 1986, as the seventy-four-year-old Lord Glenamara, he should ask me to raise his unpleasant and damaging experience of twelve years before as an issue with the Government.

The story begins on 17 July 1974, when Ted Short received a letter from Chapman Pincher, then a senior correspondent of the *Daily Express*, containing photocopies of bank documents purporting to show that Short had opened an illegal deposit account with a Swiss bank in 1971. The deputy leader of the Labour Party (as Ted Short then was) was horrified. Such a clear attempt to discredit him was plainly also an attempt to discredit the Labour Government, then about to face the second General Election within a year.

He asked the Attorney General to request the Director of Public Prosecutions to institute police inquiries. Detectives were sent to Switzerland and took two weeks to establish that the documents were forgeries, during which time they nevertheless served their purpose in creating a political furore. Harold Wilson was rightly outraged when the Opposition Chief Whip, Sir Humphrey Atkins, told his Labour counterpart that the Conservatives wanted a statement from the Deputy Prime Minister on the matter while investigations were still going on. In a memorandum to Edward Heath, drafted for Ted Short to send (which he eventually did not), Wilson expressed wholehearted disgust that 'this smear had been taken up officially by yourself and your Chief Whip . . . activities of this kind . . . are a positive threat to democracy.'[1]

After the forgery had been proved, the matter was allowed to rest, despite the failure of Scotland Yard's Serious Crimes Squad to track down its source. Lord Glenamara told me that the police, very suddenly and curiously, lost interest. Then, in December 1986, in the light of Peter Wright's disclosures, Lord Glenamara felt impelled to demand a new investigation. He now felt sure MI5 agents were responsible for forging the documents, 'no ordinary forgery', he said; 'it was a highly professional job.'

It was against this background that I wrote to the Chair-

---

[1] This memorandum is reproduced in full in the Appendix.

man of the Security Commission, the distinguished judge of the High Court, Lord Griffiths of Govilon, to request an inquiry under the 1921 Tribunals Act to consider all the alleged abuses of Labour Ministers and their staffs during the 1960s and 1970s. I listed some specific questions which seemed to me to be crucial:

1. Can it really be that the then Deputy Prime Minister of our country, a man of hitherto unquestioned integrity, was set up by a Government agency with a view to the destruction of his public life – and the consequent de-stabilising of the duly elected Government?

2. How on earth did Harry Chapman Pincher come to get hold of the expertly forged bank account, with the name changed from that of a Swiss couple to that of Mr Short? Could it have been through Mr Pincher's well-known connection with the security services, and men like Peter Wright?

3. Why did the Scotland Yard Commander and his colleagues, having been active in the case, suddenly drop it like hot bricks? Did they discover that the crime against Mr Short had been perpetrated by those working for the British State?

4. Was house-breaking, or breaking into offices, involved? If so, does such invasion of privacy, to put it mildly, take place on Ministerial authority? If not, who authorised the theft of the papers relating to a Swiss bank account?

Lord Griffiths's reply was courteous and punctilious, and I happen to know that he did indeed consult his colleagues properly and did not simply tell Rex Davie, Clerk of the Security Commission, to draft a dismissive answer. In his letter he explained that the Commission could only act as a forum for inquiry if it felt that a matter which had been referred to it warranted an inquiry, and that only the Prime Minister of the day could refer matters to it for investigation in the first place.[1]

---

[1] For Lord Griffiths's full background to the Security Commission, see Appendix.

The stumbling block was the Prime Minister. She would have none of it, and her dismissive attitude is the negation of honest Government:

Parliamentary Question 93 of Thursday 26 March 1987

Mr Tam Dalyell (Linlithgow): To ask the Prime Minister, if she will now refer to the Security Commission allegations of security services operations against Ministers of the Crown in the 1970s; and if she will make a statement.

The Prime Minister: No.

It is no startling revelation to say that the security services have their own political ends. As far back as 1924, a forged letter from Zinoviev, head of the Comintern, allegedly sent to British Communists, was leaked in an attempt to show that Labour was soft on Bolshevism.

But there is another kind of leaking of which former security officers have become past masters. The court in New South Wales has heard, at inordinate length, how the Intelligence services used trusted journalists for their own ends. The court heard how serving and retired MI5 officers had helped both Chapman Pincher and Nigel West write books about the security service, and that MI5 did nothing about it. The writing of the books was not only known about, but aided and abetted by MI5 officers and ex-officers with axes to grind or merely opinions to voice. How high in the security services this unofficial history-writing has gone is hard to say. But Mr Justice Powell had this to say about the non-banning of Pincher's book: 'I just find it very difficult . . . to think of a reason why it wasn't done. If there were no legitimate reason why it wasn't done, I would find myself pushed further and further towards the view that the Government knew exactly what was being done but wasn't going to take a step to stop it. If that was so, it is no great step to saying the Government authorised publication.'

In the case of Nigel West's book *A Matter of Trust*, one

of the ex-officers of MI5 who provided information, Arthur Martin, was identified because he confessed to having done so. Mr Justice Powell notes tersely that 'no action was taken against him and, in particular, no charges under the Official Secrets Act were laid against him'.

Now, it would be extremely foolish to suggest that the security services and this Conservative Government are in any way synonymous, or that they are acting in concert for similar ends. Yet why *has* this Government operated a double standard over secret service material, from secret service sources, which is *all* officially unpublishable?

To return to Mr Peter Wright, I do not know whether he realises the gravity of his own revelations about illegal acts by MI5 against Harold Wilson and the Labour Government. But others will certainly have understood, including some of this Prime Minister's advisers.

The law makes it clear that we are talking about treason. Since it is treason, *inter alia*, merely to (illegally) conspire to oblige the Queen to change her measures,[1] and since, under an 1848 law, it is misprision of treason to fail 'with due diligence' to inform on treasons committed or merely threatened by others, Mr Wright would seem to have an obligation to disclose the existence of any plot. One might well ask why he did not do this fifteen years ago, and inform the duly elected Labour Government – Her Majesty's Government – that it was threatened, at the time he first learned of a plot.

The Sydney court heard that there were twenty-three criminal conspiracies, twelve acts of treason, and a plot by thirty MI5 officers to destabilise the second Wilson administration, not to mention other 'deniable operations', listed in Wright's book. Another illuminating side-effect of the trial was to confirm that the Intelligence services have a section to look after political parties. I quote two

[1] R v. Lord Russell (1683) and R v. Sidney (1683).

paragraphs from the judgment: 'After he went down from Oxford, Graham Mitchell worked, for a time, as a journalist with the *Illustrated London News*, following which he worked as a statistician in the research department of the Conservative Central Office. In 1939 Graham Mitchell joined the Service.' Mr Justice Powell continues: 'Thereafter, when in 1947 or 1948, (Sir) Roger Hollis was given charge of the section concerned with the vetting of government employees and defensive, or protective, security, Graham Mitchell was given charge of the section overseeing political parties.'

I for one deeply resent the idea that democratically elected people, in local government or in the House of Commons, should be overseen by the contemporary version of Graham Mitchell, whoever he or she may be.

But more disturbing is what happened to members of the Prime Minister's entourage during the period Wright talks about. John Allen was at that time a key member of Harold Wilson's personal staff. His mother, widow of my old friend Sidney Scholfield Allen QC MP, has told me how they were burgled in extraordinary circumstances several times over that period – and John was known to be living at home. The Principal Private Secretary, Michael Halls, equally suffered burglary at his home. So did Bernard (now Lord) Donoughue. So did the press officer, Jean Denham. So did Arnold (now Lord) Goodman, the Prime Minister's solicitor.

Then there is the treatment of Lady Falkender. As Marcia Williams, she was for fifteen years a heavyweight political person – benign in my view – at the centre of Labour Party affairs. She has told me how, one evening, between the two elections of 1974, she heard running footsteps outside her home, in a London mews. Later, just before ten o'clock, her sister Peggy Field, who stayed in the house, discovered that her handbag was missing from the hall table. It contained her cheque book, keys, a valuable brooch, and less than five pounds in cash. At first the sisters thought it was a straightforward burglary of the

kind that is rife in London. But subsequent events were
to put rather a different complexion on the incident. Marcia told me that as her sister was about to call Scotland
Yard's Special Branch, the phone went and a male voice
said that he had discovered a lady's handbag. He said that
if the owner wanted it back, she would have to fetch it in
person from Bickenhall Mansions, not far from where
Marcia and her sister lived.

Feeling suspicious about the rapidity of events, Marcia
and Peggy decided that they would ask the police to collect
the bag. There was always the possibility of some kind of
unpleasant trap. When the bag was returned, all that was
missing was the cash, but the police refused to be drawn
as to the circumstances of the collection, and the inference
had to be drawn that they were acting on some kind of
higher authority. Marcia Williams also told me that her
cottage, near Great Missenden, was burgled on at least
two occasions.

As far as Peter Wright and his crew were concerned,
such operations fell into the 'deniable' category. As a
matter of habit, one precaution was taken, in case any of
the operators were caught red-handed by the police, who
would set in motion the due processes of the law before
the officer could disentangle himself. Every man engaged
in clandestine burglary carried a special pass, nicknamed
a 'Get Out of Jail Free card', familiar to the millions who
at one time or another have played Waddington's board
game of Monopoly. In the event of his being apprehended,
he could slip out of trouble by showing the magic card and
claiming that he was on 'national security business'. The
traditional English delight in grown-up schoolboy games
and shenanigans notwithstanding, this is the kind of behaviour which hitherto has been associated with Eastern
Europe, not Great Britain.

The considered view which I heard Roy Jenkins, Home
Secretary at the time of the campaign, give to the Commons's emptyish benches during the debate on the security
services on 3 December 1986 is highly relevant:

I took the view before these recent events emerged that it was advisable that MI5 should be pulled out of its political surveillance role. I had been doubtful of the value of that role for some time. I am convinced now that an organisation of people who lived in the fevered world of espionage and counter-espionage, is entirely unfitted to judge between what is subversion and what is legitimate dissent.

Nor is the associated political intelligence role worth while, in my view. The object of this is presumably to help Ministers with useful information. In my experience, however, the organisation wastes a great deal of Ministers' time in dealing with its own peccadillos, which detracts from any benefit which it provides. The balance sheet is distinctly negative.

Pontius Pilate-like, the Prime Minister says sanctimoniously, 'I can take no responsibility whatsoever for matters that happened before my time.'[1] But I am not asking her to take responsibility. What she is being asked is something quite different – and she knows full well it is different. Why will she not set up an inquiry into these events in the mid-1970s? She has no fig leaf of an excuse, since the Prime Minister of the day, Sir James Callaghan, has vouchsafed that he will co-operate.

He has intervened, with his characteristic teasing caution. Ten years previously, he ordered his own investigation into allegations that electronic devices had been planted in Number Ten Downing Street during Harold Wilson's tenure. The 1977 investigation cleared the Intelligence services of 'bugging' the Prime Minister or his staff. But to put it mildly, there is a huge question mark as to whether this review went anything like far enough to embrace the Byzantine allegations about the behaviour of sections of the security services.

Whitehall conventions mean that Mrs Thatcher has no

[1] Hansard, 17 March 1987, col. 812.

official knowledge of the 1977 investigation. Sir James says coyly that 'I am prepared to brief the Prime Minister if she wishes to consult me.' It is an odd form of words, and can only whet the appetite of curiosity. As his old friend of nearly thirty years, I take the view that if Sir James Callaghan has information of relevance and value to impart, he should pass it on; as a former Prime Minister, he is not morally entitled to sit at home, brooding on valuable evidence, and waiting for the telephone to ring.

I have evidence of my own, too, that operations against the Labour Party did not cease with the retirement of Harold Wilson. Far from it. In 1981 there was a prospect of Tony Benn becoming leader of the Labour Party and putative Prime Minister. According to Lee Tracey, an MI6 electronics expert of long experience, discussions took place in the security services and the consensus was to 'make sure Benn is stopped'. Tracey was quite clear that violent means were a possibility when he was interviewed by the *New Statesman* on 20 February 1981. Since that time I have been assured of Tracey's seriousness and factual accuracy by a source in a position to know, retired from a senior position in MI6.

Behind the back of her Attorney General, Mrs Thatcher presided over the decision-making to prosecute Peter Wright. No less has it been her decision to appeal. For legal reasons? An erstwhile tax lawyer she may be, but the weight of legal opinion is contemptuous of an appeal against Mr Justice Powell's powerful and careful judgment. No, the reasons were political. To put in the freezer, until after the 1987 General Election, any public discussion of issues raised by the Wright case.

Several times in this chapter I have pointed a cautious finger at what other shocks might be in store when the Pandora's box of the Wright case *is* opened to public discussion. By her high-handed refusal to relinquish the key which will unlock the box, the Prime Minister forces her critics to be cautious.

But if, as I believe one is entitled to, one adduces Mrs

Thatcher's stubbornly secretive behaviour as circumstantial evidence, it does not take long for it to become very clear that we are not just dealing with an alleged ill-conceived diversion of security service funds for the political ends of a freelance.group of right-wing MI5 officers. Nor are we just dealing with a list to the right in the leaky ship of MI5 and MI6 which has now been corrected. Nor are we only dealing with a Prime Minister who believes that wilfulness and strong leadership are the same thing. Intelligent conjecture can take us much further than that.

7

Dying for a Cause

This book is written out of a sense of dismay that we British nowadays too often simply shrug our shoulders at wrongdoing in public life. For example, Harry Chapman Pincher told me he already knew in the 1970s that Wilson and his entourage were bugged and burgled when he was Prime Minister, but it does not seem to have bothered him overmuch that such things should be happening to the democratically elected head of Government.

In the Falklands, brave British servicemen were asked to die, not for the national interests of Britain, but on account of the embarrassment of politicians and for the political advantage of the Prime Minister. And after British servicemen had given her victory, how she used that victory for political purposes! She claimed to the Conservative Party faithful on the Cheltenham racecourse that the Falklands had given Britain cause to abandon 'faltering and self-doubt' which had given place to 'pride and achievement'. Years later, in the United Nations, the world community, this position was supported by a vote by Oman, Belize and the Solomon Islands – but not by the United States which voted against us, nor by our European Community partners.

On the *Belgrano*, I am told by lobby correspondent upon lobby correspondent that 'we don't doubt you're right . . . but nobody's interested now . . . things have moved on . . . it's five years ago . . . it's difficult because the Navy is involved, and no one wants to read about criticism of the Navy'. It cuts little ice if I patiently explain that much of my crucial information came from naval personnel who went to the Falklands, not because of the colour of my politics, but because they felt they had been used, because some of their friends did not come back, because others came back maimed, not for the national interests of Britain, but on account of the political interests of the Prime Minister.

Not much more than a year after the Westland affair, I was saddened at the lack of political reaction to a closely-researched and trenchant TV reconstruction of the sequence of events in the leaking of the Solicitor General's letter.[1] Phoning up one political correspondent of both energy and integrity, I had the answer, 'But you see, my office think it is last year's story.' What this means in modern British politics is that a Prime Minister who can weather an immediate storm will survive. Accountability to Parliament over a longer term becomes a chimera.

On the matter of the US bombing raid on Libya, the Prime Minister's luck has held. Colonel Gadaffi has been restrained, though not by President Reagan and Mrs Thatcher, but by the soldiers of Chad. And it is worth adding that the freeing in April 1987 of the Scots engineer, Robert Maxwell, owes more to the activities of the good-hearted MP for Leith, Ron Brown, in the face of tabloid ridicule, than to any Anglo-American policies, diplomatic or military.

On the miners' strike, it is widely thought – though not in the actual coalfields of Yorkshire, Scotland and Wales – that the Prime Minister humiliated Arthur Scargill. Even the miners' president's critics know at what price and by what means. Scars in the mining communities will last for generations. But the election of Sammy Thomson, rather than Eric Clarke, to the vice-presidency of the National Union of Mineworkers suggests that many miners have

[1] Granada TV, 30 March 1987.

not rounded on Arthur Scargill, as the popular press suggest.

As to the raid on the BBC, I have been told on impeccable authority both from within the BBC and from persons in Edinburgh connected with the Scottish Office that the Secretary of State for Scotland did indeed have warning about the likelihood of a raid on Queen Margaret Drive on the Monday, *five* days before it took place. This arose because it was pointed out to police officers, busy raiding the *New Statesman* offices, that there were differences of jurisdiction between Scotland and England. Resolutely, Ministers have refused to reveal the truth about their state of knowledge.

Further, I am convinced that the genesis of the Zircon affair was all about getting rid of Alasdair Milne, then Director General of the BBC. The Prime Minister was given to understand that Mr Milne would, as she cynically hoped, go ahead and show the banned programmes, thus presenting her appointee, Mr Marmaduke Hussey, with a ready-made excuse for dismissal. (In the event Mr Milne, under unrelated personal pressures, decided to resign independently – a decision not in the original calculations of Ministers.) The entire Zircon affair had nothing to do with security of our country: had it done so, Sir Ronald Mason's and Sir Frank Cooper's notification to their former department, the Ministry of Defence, about the extent of Duncan Campbell's knowledge would not have passed unheeded for so long. Zircon was about the waving of the Prime Ministerial handbag at the BBC, and resulted in an all-too-successful attempt to bully the Corporation.

Any layman who reads Mr Justice Powell's judgment must come inexorably to the conclusion that it is a formidable and logical verdict on the Wright proceedings in the New South Wales court. Several legal luminaries, including a retired judge of the Appeal Court, have told me that they see no grounds for appeal in law against Mr Justice Powell. The appeal, at the expense of some hundreds of thousands of pounds to the British taxpayer, is an abuse and a manipulation of the law by the Prime Minister for personal purposes.

This Government has changed the ground rules, for the worse. It reflects a society in which the electorate in general expects the politicians to gull them. For the reason why Mrs Thatcher has been able to achieve this, one can do no better than turn to one of her ex-Cabinet Ministers. 'The full extent of the power of a modern Prime Minister,' said Jim Prior, 'who has the support of the Cabinet Office and Number Ten itself is still not fully appreciated. Nothing really happens in Whitehall unless the central driving force of Number Ten or the Cabinet Office has approved it.'

Sad that Prior himself took so long to realise it. Cynicism at the top has bred a cynicism to match it among the British people, which now expects its politicians to be untruthful as a matter of course. This sea-change in standards is part of the price of Mrs Thatcher's occupation of Downing Street.

I gave this chapter its title with deliberation. Since the Falklands War, all sorts of people and all sorts of principles have perished in the wake of Mrs Thatcher's actions, from the sailors on the *Belgrano* and their British opponents, to this Government's observance of the law and the accountability of the Prime Minister. They have all had one thing in common, namely that they perished in order to bolster the image and the personal power of the Rt Hon. Margaret Thatcher MP.

Some will say that these six issues are yesterday's issues, or even the day before yesterday's issues. In one sense, they would be right. Politicians tend to be like starlings going from one perch to another. Time moves on. The *dramatis personae* of public life change. Some die. Others go to the House of Lords. Others to the obscurity of private life. Those who remain in public life, like Mr Parkinson, change jobs. Accountability for yesterday's actions is difficult to pinpoint. That's why ministers get away with so much. But one minister has not been subject to retirement or musical chairs. She is the Prime Minister. And there is one aspect of the events described in this book which should not be history. That is truthfulness or non-truthfulness to the House of Commons. Those who practise deceit on the House of Commons, and when that seems to fail, go further and brazenly lie their way out of trouble (as Mrs Thatcher lied in the Westland affair), are not worthy to hold great offices of State, let alone lead this country.

Appendix

A. Sir Patrick Mayhew, the Solicitor General's letter to Michael Heseltine of 6 January 1986:

Confidential – now declassified

The Rt Hon. Michael Heseltine MP

Royal Courts of Justice

Secretary of State for Defence   London WC2A 2LL
Ministry of Defence
Main Building
Whitehall
London SW1   6 January 1986

Dear Michael,

WESTLAND

I saw in *The Times* on Saturday the text of a letter you are reported to have sent to the Managing Director of Lloyds Merchant Bank. In the course of your answer to the third question asked by Mr Horne, concerning the indications received by HMG from 'European Governments and companies' as to the projects which 'may be lost to Westland if the United Technologies/Fiat proposals are accepted', you state:

'There are indications available to HMG from both the other Governments and the companies concerned that a Westland link with Sikorsky/Fiat would be incompatible with participation by that company on

behalf of the UK in the collaborative battlefield helicopter and NH90 projects.'

This sentence, when read with the rest of the paragraph
(in which the Defence Ministers of four Governments
apart from the UK are referred to), necessarily implies
that *all* the Governments and *all* the companies involved
in the collaborative battlefield helicopter and NH90 projects have given this indication to HMG.

The telegrams (No.440 of 17 December from the Hague
and Nos. 1037 and 1083 of 5 December from Rome)
and the record of your meeting with the West German
Defence Minister in November which were available to
me when I gave advice on 31 December to the Prime
Minister on the text of her reply to Sir John Cuckney,
do not seem to me to support a statement that *all* the
Governments and *all* the companies have indicated that
a Westland link with Sikorsky/Fiat would be incompatible with participation by that company in the projects.
The documents I have seen contain evidence that the
Netherlands Defence Secretary, the German Defence
Minister and the Chairman of Agusta have commented
to the knowledge of HMG in various ways on adverse
consequences which may flow from a decision to accept
the Sikorsky offer. (In addition to Agusta, the documents disclose that Aerospatiale and MBB are addition-
ally involved in the projects.)

It is foreseeable that your letter will be relied upon by
the Westland Board and its shareholders. Consistently
with the advice I gave to the Prime Minister on 31
December, the Government in such circumstances is
under a duty not to give information which is incomplete
or inaccurate in any material particular.

On the basis of the information contained in the documents to which I have referred, which I emphasise are

all that I have seen, the sentence in your letter to Mr Horne does in my opinion contain material inaccuracies in the respects I have mentioned, and I therefore must advise that you should write again to Mr Horne correcting the inaccuracies.

I am copying this letter to the Prime Minister and to the Secretary of State for Foreign and Commonwealth Affairs, Secretary of State for Trade and Industry and the Chief Secretary of the Treasury.

Yours ever
Patrick

B. The petition and warrant for the raid on the BBC building in Queen Margaret Drive, Glasgow:

IN THE SHERIFF COURT OF GLASGOW AND STRATHKELVIN AT GLASGOW UNTO THE HONOURABLE THE SHERIFF OF GLASGOW AND STRATHKELVIN OR HIS SHERIFFS THE PETITION OF THE REGIONAL PROCURATOR FISCAL, GLASGOW AND STRATHKELVIN

GLASGOW: 31
JANUARY 1987

HUMBLY SHEWETH:

That from information received by the Petitioner it appears that the edition of the *New Statesman* magazine of 23 January 1987 contained an article entitled 'The Parliamentary Bypass Operation'.

That said article refers to information believed to be highly classified being in the possession of the British Broadcasting Corporation in connection with the preparation of a series of programmes entitled *The Secret Society*.

That there are reasonable grounds to believe that material relating to said highly-classified information has been communicated within the premises occupied by the British Broadcasting Corporation at Queen Margaret Drive, Glasgow and that evidence of said communication is retained there or in the house occupied by Wilma Purser or Paterson at 27 Hamilton Drive, Glasgow.

That said communication is in contravention of the provisions of Section 2 of the Official Secrets Act 1911 and the Petitioner has a duty to investigate the same.

The Petitioner therefore craves the court in terms of Section 9 of said Act to take the oath of James Williams, Detective Inspector of the Metropolitan Police, to the effect aforesaid and thereafter to grant warrant authorising Iain Stewart, Detective Chief Inspector of Strathclyde Police, with such assistance as he may find necessary, to enter said premises occupied by the British Broadcasting Corporation at Queen Margaret Drive, Glasgow and if necessary to use force for making such entry, whether by breaking open doors or otherwise and to search the said premises and, if necessary, every person found therein and to seize any sketch, plan, model, article, note or document or anything of a like nature, including in particular any film which is evidence of said offence under Section 2 of said Act, having been or being about to be committed, which he may find on said premises or on any such person and with regard to or in connection with which he has reasonable ground for suspecting that said offence under said Act has been, or is about to be, committed and for that purpose to seek such assistance as may be required from officials of the Ministry of Defence and to make patent all shut and lockfast places in said premises or to do further or otherwise as to your Lordship may seem meet.

ACCORDING TO JUSTICE ETC
ASSISTANT PROCURATOR FISCAL

AT GLASGOW, the 31st day of January 1987
In presence of Brian A. Lockhart Esq.,
Sheriff of Glasgow and Strathkelvin at Glasgow,
COMPEARED the said James Williams,

who being solemnly sworn and examined depones that what is contained in the foregoing Petition is true as he shall answer to God.

James Williams

Brian A. Lockhart

AT GLASGOW, the 31st day of January 1987
The Sheriff having considered the foregoing Petition and relative Oath, grants Warrant as craved.

Brian A. Lockhart

SHERIFF

C. Harold Wilson, the Prime Minister's Personal Memorandum to the Lord President, Edward Short, and the draft letter to Edward Heath which was not sent in July 1974.

10, Downing Street,
Whitehall

Prime Minister's
Personal Minute
No. . . .

LORD PRESIDENT

I enclose the draft of a letter you might consider sending
to the Leader of the Opposition. Will you please consider its wording and any alterations you would like to
make – indeed whether you are agreeable to sending it
at all – and have a word with me, when we might consider
the question of timing.

HW

On the morning of Monday, 29 July, the Government
Chief Whip informed me that on your instructions the
Opposition Chief Whip was demanding that I make a
statement in Parliament about the Zurich Bank account
smear.

I was not prepared to make such a statement since on
my own initiative I have asked the Attorney General to
call in the Police to investigate this matter, and as they
were due in Zurich at the beginning of this week, they
had asked me to make no statement whatsoever until
they reported, I was not in a position to accede to your
Party's request. Nevertheless, the pressure continued,
with threats of a Standing Order Nine Adjournment if
I made no statement before the House adjourned.

I was amazed to hear that this smear had been taken
up officially by yourself and your Chief Whip.

The action threatened by your Party was pressed
further on Tuesday last and was only averted because I
had to have a meeting with your Chief Whip after the

House assembled. I explained to him that the Chief Superintendent was in Zurich and had particularly enjoined me to make no statement.

Now that this particular smear, a characteristic product of the Dirty Tricks Department, has been officially repudiated by the Swiss National Bank, I feel entitled to ask you for an explanation of your Party's official behaviour in these pressures for a statement. If you have reason to believe that the smear was true – and it had been highly publicised in Conservative newspapers – I should be grateful if you could send me any evidence justifying your behaviour which might still be the subject of the continuing enquiries on which the Police are engaged. If you have no such evidence, I hope you will be man enough to apologise for your Party's behaviour, and also to issue a public repudiation of this and other smears which your political supporters in the Conservative press have been so assiduous in seeking to publicise.

I am making this letter available to the press, in the hope that your supporters in Fleet Street will give as much space to the truth as they gave to the lie (so far they have not done so).

I should be grateful for your early reply since activities of this kind, with which you have appeared to be only too willing to go along, are not part of a normal interchange of political debate, they are a positive threat to democracy, which the Government and the principal Opposition Parties in the House of Commons have the duty to defend.

D. The reply of the Chairman of the Security Commission, Lord Griffiths, to the request for an inquiry under the 1921 Tribunals Act into Peter Wright's allegations of illegal activities by MI5 in the mid-1970s:

House of Lords

From: The Rt Hon. the Lord Griffiths of Govilon MC

Tam Dalyell Esq MP
House of Commons
London SW1A OAA

13 January 1987

Dear Mr Dalyell

I have now had an opportunity to consult my colleagues on the content of your letter.

The Security Commission was established in 1964 in pursuant to the following statement to the House of Commons by the Prime Minister, Sir Alec Douglas Home, after consultation with the Leader of the Opposition, Mr Harold Wilson:

'If so requested by the Prime Minister to investigate and report upon the circumstances in which a breach of security is known to have occurred in the public service, and upon any related failure of departmental security arrangements or neglect of duty; and, in the light of any such investigation, to advise whether any change in security arrangements is necessary or desirable.' (Hansard cols 1271–3.)

On 10 May 1965, the Prime Minister (Mr Wilson) announced an alteration in procedure so that a reference could be made to the Commission as soon as the Government were satisfied or had reason to believe that a breach of security had occurred.

On 26 March 1969, the procedure was further modified when the Prime Minister (Mr Wilson) announced:

'After consultation with the Rt Hon. Gentleman, the Leader of the Opposition, I have revised the procedure for deciding whether or not a case involving prosecution under the Official Secrets Acts should be referred to the Security Commission. In future, when a breach of security has led to prosecution, the Chairman of the Security Commission will receive a statement outlining the facts of the case and will be asked to give his opinion on whether an investigation by the Commission would be likely to serve a useful purpose. I will then consult the Rt Hon. Gentleman taking into account the views expressed by the Chairman of the Commission before deciding whether or not to refer the case to the Commission.

In any other case of known or presumed breach of security, I would decide in the light of the circumstances whether or not its significance warranted my consulting the Chairman of the Security Commission and the Rt Hon. Gentleman on the question of whether it should be referred to the Security Commission.' (Hansard col 311.)

It is clear from these statements that the Security Commission is appointed by the Prime Minister, and that it can undertake an investigation only on a reference from the Prime Minister of the day: it has no authority to institute an investigation on its own initiative.

If, after a matter had been referred to them, the Commission were of the opinion that the powers provided by the Tribunals of Inquiry (Evidence) Act 1921 were necessary for their investigation, they would so inform the Prime Minister. It would be for the Prime Minister to seek the authority of Parliament for such powers to be granted.

Against this background, it would not be right for me or any other member of the Commission to express any opinion on your questions.

Yours sincerely
Hugh Griffiths
GRIFFITHS OF GOVILON

Index

EDNA HEALEY

WIVES OF FAME

Victorian England was a time of invention and dis-
covery, both intellectually and geographically. Three
outstanding leading figures of their generation,
Livingstone, Marx and Darwin, were the major con-
tributors to this new and exciting climate.

Each had a wife whose important role in her husband's
life has remained neglected to this day.

Now, Edna Healey, herself the wife of a major political
figure, looks at nineteenth-century history from a new
viewpoint, offering a fascinating portrait of three
remarkable women and the time in which they lived.

'The author writes with obvious integrity, and her
portraits are sympathetic and convincing'
The Times Literary Supplement

'Excellently written and researched'
The Mail on Sunday

'Fascinating reading that makes one glad to be alive
today'
Daily Telegraph

Post·A·Book

A Royal Mail service in association with the Book Marketing Council & The Booksellers Association.
Post·A·Book is a Post Office trademark.

ARTHUR GAVSHON AND DESMOND RICE

THE SINKING OF THE BELGRANO

The sinking of the *General Belgrano* on May 22 1982 was the act of war that killed off all hope of peace in the Falklands. The British nuclear submarine HMS *Conqueror* sank the Argentine cruiser with the loss of 368 lives: her two Mark 8 torpedoes also sank the delicate peace-making processes taking place in Washington and Lima to avert all-out war.

Six years later, the *Belgrano* is still in the headlines. The dark clouds of suspicion and cover-up, of misinformation and missing documents, threatens political reputations and the credibility of the British government.

NEW ENGLISH LIBRARY

JUDITH COOK

RED ALERT

Nuclear power: 'The safest form of energy
known to man'
Peter Walker, Energy Minister

That's the official line. And for thirty years most people
swallowed it. Doubters were cranks or scaremongers.

But then the reports began to build up. It slowly became clear that Windscale (hastily renamed Sellafield)
had a long history of accidents, fires, radioactive leaks.
Anxiety grew.

Then came Three Mile Island
The Sizewell 'B' Enquiry was set up. Nirex began to
roam the countryside looking for nuclear dumping
sites.

Then came Chernobyl
Now at last in *Red Alert* is the *true* history of the nuclear
power industry worldwide, the incredible record of
accident and cover-up, mismanagement and political
manipulation, of facts suppressed and downright lies.

'For far too long we have been given deceptions,
half-truths, three-quarter-truths ... This book looks
into some waters that remain too murky for the public
good'
Paddy Ashdown MP

'Has blood-curdling implications'
Books & Bookmen

NEW ENGLISH LIBRARY

JAN MOEN

JOHN MOE DOUBLE AGENT

'I handed him my pistol, and said as calmly as I could,
"We were put ashore as German spies."'

That surrender to a startled Scottish policeman in 1941
marked the start of one of the longest lasting and most
successful deceptions of World War II.

Trained by the Germans in espionage and sabotage
techniques, John Moe was to spend much of the rest of
the war on behalf of MI5, transmitting disinformation
back to his unsuspecting German 'controllers'.

He travelled the length and breadth of Britain. He
reported on troop movements and military equipment.
He even seemingly carried out acts of sabotage. His
reports played a major part in convincing the Germans
that Norway rather than Normandy would be the
objective of the Allied Invasion of 1944 – so keeping
thousands of enemy troops tied down uselessly in the
wrong place.

Now living quietly in Sweden, John Moe has told for
the first time the extraordinary story of his wartime life
as a double agent.

NEW ENGLISH LIBRARY

NIGEL WEST

MOLEHUNT

In May 1951 Guy Burgess and Donald Maclean slipped hurriedly out of the country. Within days they had reached Moscow. From that day to this, the British Security Service has been in torment.

Somebody had tipped the traitors off.

Evidence of Maclean's duplicity had been accumulated over a long period but, just when MI5 was about to intercept him, he fled. Only a limited number of counter-intelligence officers knew of the plan to question Maclean, so the field was limited.

The hunt for the mole was on.

From that day to this a whole series of top-level investigations has followed. Names have been suggested, oblique accusations made, mistrust has eaten away at the morale of the organisation but the truth has never been revealed.

Until now. Nigel West has answered the questions and the results are stranger than any fiction and twice as compelling.

CORONET BOOKS

MORE NON-FICTION FROM
HODDER AND STOUGHTON PAPERBACKS